The MYSTERY FANcier

Volume 9, Number 3
May/June 1987

The Mystery Fancier

Volume 9, Number 3
May/June 1987

TABLE OF CONTENTS

The Mystery Fancier
(USPS: 428-590)
is edited and published by-monthly by
Guy M. Townsend
407 Jefferson Street
Madison, IN   47250

SUBSCRIPTION RATES: Second-class mail, U.S. and Canada,
$15.00 per year (6 issues); first-class mail, U.S. and Canada,
$18.00; overseas surface mail, $15.00; overseas air mail, $21.00.
Overseas subscribers please pay in international money order,
check drawn on U.S. bank, or currency; no checks drawn on
foreign banks, please.

WILDSIDE PRESS

Mysteriously Speaking ...

I don't have to point out to you folks that this issue is late. And I won't bore you with the details of why it is; you've heard them all before from me. I do have something new to say, however, and it relates to the future of TMF.

As many of you know, the editorial and production aspect of TMF has always, with the exception of the Minnesota experiment a few years back, been a one-man operation. I do what little editing is actually done to the copy, I feed it into the computer keystroke by keystroke (except when some lovely soul sends a disk along with the hard copy), I do the paste-ups and the camera work, operate the offset press, collate, fold, and staple, stuff and address the envelopes, and drag the whole thing down to the post office every couple of months—all of which takes considerable amounts of time, a commodity which is in increasingly short supply around here. So short, in fact, that if I can't find some way of economizing on my expenditure of time I'm going to have to let TMF die at the end of the current volume.

I've been thinking about it, and the only way I've been able to come up with to make it possible for me to continue with TMF after this year is to rid myself of the production details—the camera work, printing, collating, binding, etc. If I didn't have all that to attend to, I think that I would be able to find enough time not only to keep TMF alive but even to improve on my editorial performance, which has become somewhat slipshod of late (not that it was ever much to write home about). Now, I invested thousands of dollars setting up my own print shop just so that I could keep production costs down by doing all the work myself, and if I farm the work out it's going to cost a good deal more than when TMF was being printed essentially for the cost of paper and ink. I've looked into the situation, and I've decided that the most practical and economical solution would be to change TMF from a bi-monthly to a quarterly publication and to change the format from its present saddle-stapled configuration to a classier perfect bound, trade paperback format. The new, quarterly TMF would be at least twice the size of the issue you are now reading—the actual page count would be between 100 and 112 pages, which I have not yet settled with the printer.

These four quarterly issues, in their more expensive format
and totalling 400-448 pages per year, would have to cost more
than the present TMF, with its annual count of 300 pages. To
be specific, the annual subscription rate (second class) would
have to increase from the current rate of $15.00 to a new rate
of $25.00 for me to be able to afford to carry on. (The single
issue price would skyrocket from $3.00 to $7.50.) First class
subscriptions would increase to $30.00 per year, and overseas air
mail subscriptions, which I have been subsidizing for years,
would have to begin to pay their own way and would go to
$35.00 per year. (Overseas surface subscriptions would be the
same as domestic second class subscriptions: $25.00.)

These figures are based on TMF having a subscription base
of at least two hundred. If fewer than two hundred of you are
willing to subscribe to TMF volume ten at these rates, then I
won't be able to afford to have someone else print it; and, since
I can no longer afford the time it takes to print it myself, TMF
will have to fold its tent for good at the end of this year.

So be thinking about it, folks, and let me know as soon as
possible whether you'll be willing to fork over the additional
tariff. To make it easier for TMF's domestic subscribers to
make their wishes known on this matter, I am enclosing pre-
addressed postcards in this issue; just write "yes" or "no" on the
card, add your name and address, and then drop it back in the
mail to me as soon as possible. If I have received two hundred
positive responses before I put out TMF 9:6--which, believe it
or not, I still hope to get out in December of this year--I'll
announce TMF's continuance by enclosing a renewal form with
that issue. If, on the other hand, fewer than two hundred of
you express your willingness to pay the steeper price, TMF will
come to an end with 9:6 (and I'll finally have time to start
catching up on the reading I haven't had time for since starting
TMF up in November 1976).

One of the side benefits of going to a quarterly publication
schedule would be that the larger issue size would make it
possible to run longer articles in TMF--articles such as Maryell
Cleary's piece on clerical detectives which takes up so much
space in this issue. Maryell thoughtfully suggested running the
article in parts, but I thought it was stronger as a whole so
here it is.

I've sent copies of my first two booklists to all TMF
subscribers, but subsequent lists will go only to people who have
purchased from previous lists or who have specifically requested
that they be placed on my catalog mailing list. If you are
interested, be sure you let me know.

Special--albeit quite belated--congratulations to our own
Bob Sampson for the Edgar he won for his *New Black Mask*
short story "Rain in Pinton County." Bob really has a magical
way with words, and it's about time he was getting the consideration he deserves.

Contemporary Clergy-Detectives

Maryell Cleary

On the shelves of bookstores and libraries these days are books featuring a remarkable lot of clergy who detect on the side: priests, nuns, ministers, and rabbis. Unlike Chesterton's classic, Father Brown, they are deeply involved with what is going on in contemporary religious life. Father Brown was a figure out of time, a lone priest without parish, bringing his moral precepts and insights to the detection of crime. The Roman Catholic Church as a major worldwide institution had little, if anything, to do with his activities. Unlike Tony Boucher's Sister Ursula, the contemporary clergy-detectives are not separated from the world in a cloister. Sister Ursula could go out only with a nun-companion, and for her the possibility of helping detect a murderer could be the occasion of the sin of pride. Today's clergy-detectives are immersed in the world; they cannot escape involvement in whatever is going on there. Religion, in these contemporary mystery novels, is inextricably entwined with such worldly horrors as drug abuse, terrorism, poverty, the plight of refugees, and the excesses of greed and cruelty. The clergy are not portrayed as saints; they too have sinned. Religion, these authors are saying, is not only relevant to life, it is life.

In this article I will survey the several series of books about clerical detectives now being written. There are books about other clergy-detectives available occasionally in libraries, notably those of Margaret Scherf about Episcopalian Father Martin Buell, and Leonard Holton's Father Bredder, but so far as I know these are no longer continuing series. Those authors now writing have created a variety of clergy: three Roman Catholic priests and two nuns of that faith, one Anglican priest, one Episcopalian woman priest, one main-line Protestant minister, and two rabbis. Conspicuously missing are funda-mentalist or evangelical Protestant clergy, women ministers and rabbis, and representatives of smaller faith groups, such as the Greek Orthodox or the Moslem, Buddhist, and Hindu groups now active in this country. Protagonists from the liberal religious groups are also missing; there are no Reform or Reconstruc-tionist rabbis, no Unitarian Universalist ministers, no leaders of humanist groups or Ethical Societies. So there's still plenty of room in the field for more!

I. The Roman Catholic Priests

Father Brown was a priest on his own. He held no parish pastorate, hobnobbed with no priest friends, rarely said Mass for any flock, and seemed to be answerable to no one above him in the hierarchy. His Roman Catholic background and priestly way of thinking helped him to understand human foibles and sins, but he did so without a church context.

Today's priest-detectives are firmly fixed within the Roman Catholic Church structure. They exemplify the post-Vatican Church in its variety, its trends, and its conflicts. Three priests have thus far appeared as series detectives: Ralph McInerny's Father Roger Dowling, William Kienzle's Father Robert Koesler, and Andrew Greeley's Monsignor John Blackwood Ryan. They are very different people, holding very different places in the Church. Their authors, naturally, are as varied as their creations. McInerny is not a priest, but a Professor of Philosophy at Notre Dame University. He is a prolific writer in both fiction and nonfiction fields. Kienzle is a former priest, for a number of years editor of a Catholic publication in the Archdiocese of Detroit. He left the priesthood, married, and was for a time director of a Center for Contemplative Studies; he is now a full-time writer living in the Detroit area. Andrew Greeley is both priest and sociologist. He has written exten- sively about the Roman Catholic Church, and he is now writing popular fiction which brings in a great deal of money; much of this he has contributed to Catholic causes. All three authors are experts on the state of the Roman Catholic Church in America in the 1980s.

Father Roger Dowling

In Father Roger Dowling, Ralph McInerny has created a pastoral priest, a human being who has erred, who can therefore understand and forgive repentant sinners. He is above all concerned with mercy, repentance, and forgiveness. Dowling's background makes his concerns believable. He was one of the Church's coming men, one of those from whom bishops are made. He was an expert on canon law and spent fifteen years on the Marriage Tribunal in Chicago. This was a heartbreaking task. Every day he tried to apply both justice and mercy to the tortured men and women who came to him seeking release from already broken marriages. He knew that the process he began for them was almost always doomed to failure; they would have to choose between staying in the church and their marriages, or leaving both marriage and church. To make that knowledge easier to live with, Dowling began to drink. Only a little at first, then a gradual increase until he was an alcoholic. Finally he blacked out. There followed a stay at a place for priestly alcoholics in Wisconsin, drying out. But his career was finished, and, truly, he did not care. He asked for a parish and received St. Hilary's, a declining parish in Fox River, a Chicago exurb. Once St. Hilary's was a large and thriving parish; now its area has been cut up by expressways, its numbers decimated. Its parochial school is closed, turned into a day care center for the elderly and those with nowhere to go. For Father Dowling it is salvation. At fifty he starts a new life.

He is essentially a pre-Vatican II priest. He reads his breviary daily; he hears confessions in a confessional booth rather than in the new, open style. He regrets the loss of Latin, but he is obedient to church authority. He has an old-fashioned housekeeper, Marie Murkin, who pampers him in spite of his efforts to resist. Most important, in St. Hilary's parish he finds a friend.

Policeman Phil Keegan spent a year at Quigley Preparatory Seminary, the high-school-level training school leading to the priesthood, from which Dowling graduated and went on. But Phil couldn't master Latin and flunked out. He married and is now a widower, with two daughters who live far away. He has a satisfying career in the Fox River police department, though he constantly is frustrated by the corruption at the top. He lives in an apartment, his work his life—until Roger Dowling comes to Fox River and they become friends. They play pinochle together, watch Cubs games, Phil drinking beer, Roger smoking cigars, Marie making popcorn for them.

Phil, first Inspector, then Captain, shares his cases with Roger. Dowling can be trusted and is interested from a different point of view. Keegan represents justice; he's concerned with catching criminals and bringing them to trial. Dowling represents mercy; he's concerned with souls and is always hoping to bring murderers to repentance and absolution. He thinks of another life beyond this one for those condemned to die.

St. Hilary's may be a backwater, but Fox River has many of the same problems as large cities. Some of them come from the nearest large city, Chicago. Organized crime has spread out to the exurbs and in Fox River controls the police chief and a thriving drug traffic. The deadly sins of lust, greed, gluttony, and others are apparent in the smaller city just as in the large one. They enter into the crimes which Keegan must solve.

Several continuing characters spice the books. There is Tuttle, the crooked lawyer, incompetent and greedy, who provides comic relief and gets in the way of both the good guys and the bad. There is "Peanuts" Pianone, on the police force because of his powerful mob family, but so dumb as to be funny. There is Agnes Lamb, black policewoman, whose presence allows the author to deal with both sexism and racism. There are Mervel and Wiggins, newspaper reporter and television news star respectively, whose rivalries are laughable and yet recognizable as similar to those in larger cities. Marie Murkin continues through the series, sometimes taking a major role.

The Father Dowling books are Roman Catholic at a basic, personal level. Since Dowling hears confessions, he sometimes hears about a crime that's been committed and is unable to tell Keegan. He has to hope that the police will get the information in some other way, and sometimes he can help on that without breaking the seal of the confessional. His daily responsibilities as a priest often enter into the solving of a crime. In one novel, he notices the absence of one regular attender from the lightly attended noon Mass, and he investigates. As a priest he can go where others could not without suspicion, and that can be useful. He can also draw morals and garner insights into human behavior.

In the first book, *Her Death of Cold*, he muses, "How often the deed we mean to do turns into something else, something we did not really intend. A relatively innocent action, an instinctive response, can look to the outsider like a criminal deed.... A priest learns how frequently sinful deeds can wear an innocent public face. The outward consequences, the observable effects of what we do are seldom commensurable with the true nature of our acts." (pp. 243-244)

When the bishop comes to Fox River, it is to perform confirmations, not to talk church politics. When, in *Bishop as Pawn*, the bishop is kidnapped, he is shown as a frightened and hungry human being, not as a Prince of the Church. The results of Vatican II, who's going to be made a bishop or a cardinal, the decisions of the Pope, all of these seem far away and not very important at St. Hilary's. The Church goes on as it always has, a vehicle for daily life. And among that daily life is crime, murder, and sin, with which Roger Dowling is uniquely prepared to cope. Through his inside information about his people and their ways, and about Catholics in general, he can often find the solutions to crimes while Keegan handles the routine. Together they make an unbeatable team.

Father Robert Koesler

The author of the novels about Father Robert Koesler, William Kienzle, was a priest for twenty-four years. Fourteen of those were spent as editor of the *Michigan Catholic.* His first novel, *The Rosary Murders*, published in 1979, was an instant success; it has now been made into a movie, and Kienzle has gone on writing mysteries about his priest-protagonist.

Koesler follows Kienzle's own career footsteps up to a point. He is based in Detroit; in the first book he is editor of the *Detroit Catholic;* later he is attached to a parish. Unlike Father Dowling, Koesler is gregarious. He is often with his priest-colleagues, playing golf, having lunch and dinner, almost endlessly eating, drinking, smoking, and cracking jokes about church and clergy.

Like Father Dowling, he has a police detective friend. During the course of *The Rosary Murders* he comes to know and like then-Lieutenant Walter Kosnicki, and the feeling is mutual. The friendship is strong and carries on through the continuing roster of murder cases on which they collaborate. Kosnicki, though, is a married man, so he does not have empty hours to spend with Koesler.

As seen through Koesler's eyes, the Roman Catholic Church is a very different institution than the one Roger Dowling lives with every day. It is a worldwide institution encompassing many

others. Readers of the Father Koesler series will become well
acquainted with some of those smaller Institutions in the Detroit
area. Rich churches in the suburbs, poor ones In the inner city,
seminaries nearly devoid of students, newspapers reporting
church news, hospitals, parochial schools, rectories housing
assorted priests, are all there. This is a Church In post-Vatican
II turmoil. The priests and nuns react to this in their own
individual ways, some by refusing to admit that there has been
any change, others by embracing it. There are priests like
Father Farmer, who gives the same Lenten sermons he's given
for years, still emphasizing the fear of hell. There are nuns
who say the same prayers in the same old way, while regretting
that they aren't allowed to give the sacraments as priests do.
There are those who reminisce about the good old days when
"Father" was the undisputed authority in his parish, and those
who welcome the opening of the church to greater lay participa-
tion.

One book, *Assault with Intent*, is set largely in the
seminaries of the Detroit area. This allows Kienzle to expatiate
on the shortage of priests and seminarians. He takes readers to
Sacred Heart Seminary, where candidates for the priesthood are
so scarce that some are allowed to stay who would have been
summarily shunted out in the old days. In the same novel he
takes us into a group of Catholics who long for Tridentine
times, pre-Vatican II, when the Mass was said In Latin.

As an old newspaper editor, Kienzle likes to depict
reporters. Two of his continuing characters are Pat Lennon and
Joe Cox, reporters for the *Free Press* at the outset, then on
rival newspapers. As they are also live-in lovers, this can cause
some problems. So far the honors are about even; they're both
top-notch at their jobs, and both are always involved in
reporting the progress of the murder cases in which Father
Koesler is involved. Their personal relationship and professional
rivalry add a realistic and lively touch to the novels.

Kienzle is intensely interested in the politics of the post-
Vatican II Church. His bishops and archbishops are indeed
Princes of the Church, deferred to for their authority and
power, though it's clear that neither is as great as they used to
be. Priests still get special treatment from the public in these
books, not always deservedly. They are not shown as specially
spiritual people; indeed, we see how often they are avid for
creature comforts, and how rare is the one with a real spiritual
life, who can inspire his parishioners to be better people.

Though much has changed in the Church Kienzle portrayed,
some things remain the same. The confessional is sacred, and
what a priest hears there cannot be told to anyone. Modern
Father Koesler feels just as bound by this as the more old-
fashioned Father Dowling. But he is, in the main, a liberal. He
believes that divorce is sometimes a necessity, and that women
should be ordained to the priesthood. At the same time he
thinks that the vernacular Mass is a mistake; the quality of the
English texts is poor, and the mystery of the Latin is gone. He
laments that the Gregorian chant is only a memory and says
that the new liturgical music is puerile. In one place he says,

of the Church's marriage laws, that "the laws of the Church are antithetical to the law of Christ." Nevertheless he sticks to his Church and his vocation.   However much he may ridicule priests, he is compassionate and caring towards them and devoted to the long-term welfare of the Roman Catholic Church.

Kienzle's books are action-packed. He creates series of crimes, and in a few books series of possible solutions. Though this smacks of gimmickry, it makes possible large casts of characters and a variety of locales. The routine detection is done by the police. Father Koesler is called in when it is clear that his expertise as a priest can be useful. His understanding of the motives of individual Catholics is often the key to the solution of a long series of murders. The locale of church, rectory, and seminary brings him into cases and so does the identity of victims. One of the recent books, however, takes him out of his own milieu into the Detroit Cougars' pro football team, when its star player dies suddenly and mysteriously. Since Koesler is a member of the "God Squad," a Bible-study group to which the player belonged, he has an inside track. As usual, his knowledge of the Church and its people bring the case to a successful conclusion.

As Kienzle's books move away from the politics and places of the Roman Catholic Church, one wonders if his priest-detective will follow his author out of the priesthood, marry, and move into secular employment. If so, we would then be reading about an ex-priest-detective, the first of his kind.

Monsignor John Blackwood Ryan

Monsignor Ryan, "Blackie" to most everyone, was created by the priest-author, Father Andrew Greeley. Greeley is well-known as the prolific author of best-selling non-mystery novels and as a sociologist and professor. Blackie, his priest-detective, has thus far starred in two novels in a series based on the Beatitudes from the Gospel of St. Matthew.

Blackie is the rector of Holy Name Cathedral, which is the residence of the Cardinal Archbishop of the archdiocese of Chicago, Sean Cronin. Ryan was born and brought up in the well-to-do Irish enclave in southside Chicago, Beverly. He has ties with the wealthy and influential and has no need to feel awe in the presence of Richard Daley, Jr., son of the late mayor of the city. Greeley knows this background well. The people in these novels are the Irish who have made it into the city's upper echelons, and even far beyond the city: in the police, the priesthood, at the bar, in business, and as far away as Hollywood. Though they have gone far, they have never outgrown their Catholic upbringing entirely. They have direct access to Cardinal Cronin, but he refers their offbeat problems to Blackie, who enjoys investigation more than his regular pastoral duties. Fortunately, he has plenty of young assistants to do the chores of saying Mass and hearing confessions.

Greeley says that the interpretation of the Beatitudes which he uses in these books is now an orthodox one, though it's by no means the one most lay people would endorse. In *Happy Are the Meek*, the first book, the "meek" person is the wife of the murdered man. She has been meek in the usual sense of the term all her life, obeying her husband in all things, trying to keep her family together in the face of his alcoholism and aberrant behavior. She only becomes "happy" when she rebels and refuses his last, outrageous order. That night he dies in his locked study, whether by accident or at someone's hand is not at first clear. Blackie is called in by the man who loves the now-widowed Suzie Quinlan, Lawrence F.X. Burke. Suzie is being haunted by noises and manifestations which she thinks are her husband's way of demanding Catholic burial. As he had become part of a Satanist cult before his death, he could not be buried in consecrated ground. Burk wants an exorcism—or something. The something turns out to be an investigation of Wolfe Tone Quinlan's death by Blackie, who drags the whole miserable, nasty family history out into the light and at long last finds out the truth of how he died.

In the second book, *Happy Are the Clean of Heart*, the "clean of heart" are those who are not envious of the talents and treasures of others. Few in this book measure up, save Lisa Malone, the victim of a brutal, torturing, murderous attack. It is clear that only one of her close friends, co-workers, or her husband could have done it. Blackie, who has loved Lisa since their childhood in the same neighborhood and parochial school, again investigates. Lisa is so good, so beautiful, so talented, so loving, that she could almost apply for sainthood. She makes lots of money and outshines other Hollywood stars with whom she works. Now she has made a new film, directing and producing it herself, which she believes will be revolution-ary. Everyone in her entourage claims to be outraged by the attack and protests great love for Lisa. Each of them, however, wants something from her. Some of them are cheating her, all of them are envious of her. From a considerable cast of likely suspects Blackie must pick the right one, before he or she strikes again.

Greeley proved in his earlier, non-mystery best-sellers that he could write steamy sex combined with violence. He has carried this ability with him into his mysteries. For readers nostalgic for the Golden Age he also provides maps and diagrams and lists of characters. In the first book the publisher has added a questionaire which allows the reader to respond to questions about whether or not there's too much sex, too much violence, and if the book gives the reader a sense of the love of God or not. For Greeley insists that he is writing about the love of God. As he wrote in his recent autobiography, *Confes-sions of a Parish Priest*, "They [the novels] are stories of 'epiphanies' of 'breaking in' of God to the ordinary events of human life." He refers to his novels as "comedies of grace." He finds the love of God exemplified par excellence in human sexuality; unfortunately, one has to wade through a great deal of angry, cruel, drunken, lecherous, ungodly sex in order to get to a very short epiphany.

Blackie has a friend on the Chicago police force, Mike

Casey the cop, always referred to in that way. Most of the time, though, Blackie goes it alone. He calls on Mike Casey the cop when police assistance is absolutely necessary. There's very little sharing of information or friendly, relaxed rap sessions. Greeley tells his stories in short chapters in which each of the characters speaks in his or her own words. This gives readers the opportunity to check them against each other and to do a little detecting themselves.

Readers of the Father Dowling and Father Koesler books learn quite a bit about the contemporary Roman Catholic Church, from two quite different view points. Readers of the Monsignor Ryan books learn about the Irish Catholic community and its people's response to their Catholic identity rather than about the Church itself. Another, and not uninteresting, point of view.

II. The Roman Catholic Nuns

The Roman Catholic nuns in contemporary mystery fiction are post-Vatican II just as the priests are. Gone are the days when Sister Ursula had to have a chaperon-companion, another nun, with her at all times when she was out of the convent. It's not so much that today's nuns are a different breed, as that they live in a different world. They are still devoted to their religion and to the work they do. They are still bound by vows of poverty, chastity, and obedience. Obedience may be somewhat more broadly interpreted, but chastity is not and none of these women lives high on the hog.

Today's nuns, most of them, live in the secular community, working, going to school, studying, being of service. They do not cohabit with men, but men are always on the scene, part of their daily lives. Except for older women who don't want to change the ways of most of a lifetime, they don't wear traditional habits but dress quietly in contemporary style. Their devotions do not impinge greatly on the readers' attention. They live in small groups or in college communities rather than in cloisters. They are rather ordinary women living ordinary lives, but to whom extraordinary things happen. Ralph McInerny, writing under the pseudonym of Monica Quill, has chronicled several adventures of Sisters Mary Theresa, Joyce, and Kimberley. Sister Carol O'Marie is two books into a series featuring Sister Mary Helen.

Sister Mary Teresa Dempsey

There are only three nuns left in the Order of Mary and Martha, a once-thriving order with a college of its own. The three live in a Frank Lloyd Wright house on Walton Street in Chicago. When the order modernized, it sold all its property and gave the money to the poor, leaving only this house and one at the Indiana Dunes. Elderly Sister Mary Teresa Dempsey, inevitably called "Emtee Dempsey" behind her back, a scholar who is writing a definitive work on twelfth-century monasticism, continues to wear the old habit with its wings of white about the face and its full black robe. Sister Kimberley Moriarty is working on her Ph.D. at Northwestern University and serves as Emtee's research assistant. In solving mysteries she is Emtee's eyes, ears, and legs. Sister Joyce is their housekeeper, and, though a secret smoker, is more like an old-fashioned nun than the other two. Kim's brother Richard is on the Chicago police force.   He consistently appears in each book, usually in an angry mood because the nuns are interfering in police work—again.

The menage is much like that of Nero Wolfe.   Emtee is heavy and somewhat dictatorial. She sends Kim out to do the investigating for her. Kim is outgoing, smart, and gutsy, though she's sometimes appalled at what Emtee asks her to do.   Joyce fills the role of Fritz Brenner, though not with gourmet cooking, while Richard has much in common with Inspector Cramer, often angry at these amateurs who withhold information.   Emtee is even like Nero Wolfe in liking to get all the suspects together in the last chapter, to go over the evidence, spring her conclusions, and unveil the murderer.

The house on Walton Street sometimes harbors people the police are looking for; Sister Mary Teresa does her own interrogating in her own study, while Kim is out in the more dangerous position of letting suspects know that they are suspected. Joyce is the quiet foil for the other two. The Order of Mary and Martha goes on, seriously depleted, and Kim wonders what will happen to it when Sister Mary Teresa dies. But that won't be for a while yet; McInerny-Quill obviously has in mind an ongoing series.

Sister Mary Helen

Sister Mary Helen, created by a nun, Sister Carol O'Marie, is the latest addition to the ranks of nun-detectives.   Mary Helen has turned seventy-five in the first book, *A Novena for Murder.* She's one of the old breed who has taken to the new ways with zest. Sadly, she has come to the end of her career as a teacher; however, O'Marie is giving her one or two more careers for her later years. There's lots of life left in Sister Mary Helen!

She has been retired to Mount St. Francis College for Women in San Francisco, her alma mater. At first she is assigned to do historical research; in the second book, *Advent of Dying*, she is running the alumnae office.   An old friend, Sister Eileen, is the college librarian, and a new friend, the young nun-chaplain, Sister Anne, becomes another colleague in the solving of mysteries.

Mary Helen turns into an engagingly curious amateur detective when she finds the dead body of the head of the history department, Professor Villanueva. He has been engaged in the humanitarian work of sponsoring Portuguese immigrants to this country.   Several of them work for the college, but several others have recently disappeared. These events are not unrelated, as Mary Helen discovers when she begins to talk to the families of those who disappeared.

Naturally there is a connection with the police department. A Mount St. Francis alumna, Inspector Kate Murphy, and her partner, Inspector Dennis Callahan, are assigned to the case. Though Mary Helen's personal investigation often irritates them, they can't get her to stop, and eventually they have to admit that she's being helpful. The two detectives are to be continuing characters in the series, it seems, as they also appear in the second book. Kate's private life is a story of its own, parallel to the murder cases, and it's influenced more than she'd like to say by the good sister's words and attitudes.

This nun is not at all inactive. She's out in the San Francisco streets, in fog and sunshine, by car and on foot. She talks to everyone connected with the cases, and she seeks out some the police haven't yet interviewed. At times this makes people mad at her; at times it's frustrating for her, and at other times frustrating for the police.

The second book, *Advent for Dying*, also takes place on the college campus, when another of Sister Mary Helen's coworkers is murdered. This book takes Mary Helen and some other sisters to a night spot where exotic dancers perform and into an apartment building inhabited by some very odd people. The good sister worries about the case and just won't let go until she has solved it. She is strangely oblivious to the fact that she is a threat to murderers and blithely goes off on her own, putting herself in grave danger from which she has to be rescued.

Sister Mary Helen is a very likeable person; her intelligence, her concern for people, her determination to get to the bottom of each mystery—all come through. However, she could be any seventy-five-year-old unmarried woman who's had a satisfying career and is seeking other things to do to make her life meaningful. There is little in the books that speaks to the religious life or to the Catholic Church and its changes. Sister Anne, the college chaplain, with her posters, floor pillows, and incense, is the closest thing to a statement about changes that the author makes. Only in the relationship of Mary Helen with Kate Murphy does a Catholic theme show up; Mary Helen still looks on marriage and child-bearing as the best, most natural state for women, and she gently nudges Kate in that direction. One can only hope that Kate's police career will not have to come to an end.

III. The Protestants

The Rev. Claire Aldington

Claire Aldington is one of a fast-growing new group of clergy, the women Episcopal priests. She is the only ordained woman to figure as an amateur detective thus far. Her creator,

Isabelle Holland, has written a number of romantic novels as
well as two mysteries starring Aldington and one in which she
appears as a background character. Aldington is a pastoral
counselor on the staff of a large church in New York City, St.
Anselm's.

The two books featuring Aldington as detective give
readers a vivid picture of the conflict felt in many big city
churches over their role in the modern world. In a city where
poverty is rife, street people abundant, the homeless growing in
numbers, what should the church be doing? How should its
finite resources be allocated? How can the church serve both
its affluent constituents and the poor for whom religion may
seem irrelevant? Conflicts such as these are at the heart of
the novels Holland writes about Aldington, even though romance
also plays an important part in them.

St. Anselm's has a shelter for the homeless and a soup
kitchen in its building; it reaches out to those who "live" on the
street corner opposite. Its staff has to cope not only with
these people and their problems, but also with the concerns of
its well-to-do members, who don't want to get rid of all the
church's assets in order to feed and house the poor.

In the first book, *Death at St. Anselm's*, the homeless who
sleep in the shelter are the first suspects when Dick Grism,
paraplegic business manager of the church, is killed in his
office. They are soon ruled out, however, and suspicion falls on
members of the church staff. There are plenty of suspects, as
this is a multiple-staff church, with assistant rectors, rector,
intern seminarian, and a full complement of office and custodial
staff, as well as Claire in her job as pastoral counselor. She
becomes a prime suspect, and later on her step-daughter joins
her in this unenviable position.

Claire is a thirty-five-year-old widow. Her husband,
Patrick, was also a clergyperson. He was killed in an auto-
mobile accident. Claire lives with their young son, Jamie, and
her teen-age step-daughter, Martha, who is neurotic and
anorexic. With the help of Brett Cunningham, wealthy business-
man and volunteer business manager for the church, Claire
begins to investigate the crime. The police lieutenant never
becomes a friend, but in the course of the books he does
become less suspicious of Claire and more willing to cooperate
with her.

In this first book there is quite heavy emphasis on a new
romance for Claire and the discovery she makes about her late
husband which leads to a reevaluation of their marriage.

A Lover Scorned again stars Aldington as amateur detective
in the killing of another woman priest. She is drawn into the
investigation by the police, who think that she may have access
to information about the woman which they cannot otherwise
get. As Claire presses her inquiries, she learns more about
other churches in her city, especially about a small one whose
rector is anti-Establishment in sympathy with his slum-dwelling
parishioners. The inner conflicts of the Episcopal Church are
again vividly shown.

A new rector at St. Anselm's is from England, making clear

the close connection that exists between the Episcopal Church
in this country and the Church of England. Male priests move
easily from one country's churches to those of the other.
Women priests are still not accepted in England, but, again, this
factor is not stressed in these books.

A bag lady whose "home" is on the street corner opposite
St. Anslem's is sympathetically treated in *A Lover Scorned*. She
hallucinates that she's protecting England from attack and
refuses to take the medication that would keep her in a more
"normal" state. There's method in this madness, however: her
beloved cat-companion isn't welcome anywhere else but on the
street corner, and she won't give him up in order to live in a
shelter or some kind of home arranged by her relatives.
Claire's assistance to her in the cat's illness provides insight
into Claire's character and sets up some of the plot's convo-
lutions.

The romantic element is strong in this book, too, as Claire
finds herself jealous of her fiance's past involvement with the
murdered woman. However, the book is essentially a mystery.
More murders are committed; detection is done; a frightening
kidnapping twists the plot another turn. With some help from
the fiance, Aldington unmasks the culprit.

Holland's plots are complex and her characters real. The
religious institution in which her major characters operate faces
the real problems and dilemmas of churches in large cities these
days. Ultimately, only the question of who did the murdering is
resolved; the larger question of the church's role in society has
to be left open-ended, just as it is in real life.

The Rev. Simon Bede

Simon BEde is a priest of the Church of England. He is a
troubleshooter for the Archbishop of Canterbury, a sort of
fictional Terry Waite, though conceived before Waite became a
celebrity. He was created by Barbara Ninde Byfield and Frank
Tedeschi, who dared each other to write a mystery when they
were on the vestry of St. Luke's in the Fields, New York City.
Byfield had written and illustrated several children's books,
while Tedeschi had been trained in journalism as well as in
liturgy. The collaboration worked well and both enjoyed it, says
Byfield, but they were not able to continue as collaborators
because of the heavy workload Tedeschi has as head of com-
munications for the Episcopal Church. Byfield has continued the
series on her own, with Bede appearing, sometimes only periph-
erally, in three more books. His close woman-friend, Helen
Bullock, free-lance photographer, has gradually taken on the
major role.

The first book, *Solemn High Murder*, is set in the Church
of St. Jude the Martyr, in New York. Since the architecture of
the church is important to the plot, it is good that the authors
provide a floor plan to guide the reader. The side chapel where
a small group of charismatics hold their arcane rituals, the
organist's niche, the corner back of a screen where the rector,

Dunstan Owsley, hears confessions, all are shown so that we can visualize the action within its scene. Like St. Anselm's, this is another large church in a large city, with multiple staff and many active lay people.

Bede, fresh from a mission to a very poor parish in the Caribbean, has stopped off in New York to visit Owsley and offer him a higher position in the Anglican Church. When murder occurs, Simon is the only person who is both knowledge-able about church affairs and somewhat objective. He also has an easy entree to all the diverse people and groups within the church. He is able to assess the possible motives of the granddaughter of the church's wealthiest parishioner, her hippy boyfriend and their group of charismatics, the assistant rector who wants a more remunerative and responsible position, the anonymous writer of a book about a Black Mass, and sundry others. As the book progresses, Simon Bede meets Helen Bullock, professional photographer and independent woman, who becomes his lover and companion.

In the later books Simon moves into retirement from his clergy position. He could be called back to duty by the Archbishop, but that doesn't happen. None of the other books have church settings. The second is set in a Michigan summer community where a few families have had homes for many years. Helen is on her own, visiting her aged greatuncle and the people she grew up with. Simon appears only in letters.

In the third book, *A Harder Thing Than Triumph*, Simon and Helen are travelling together in the Berkshires. They are visiting a distant cousin of Simon's on a semi-retirement farm community when Helen falls prey to a youngster's trick and breaks a bone in her foot. This strands them there for a while and involves them in a mysterious death and a disappearance. Here Simon plays a priestly role, though not as a dispenser of sacraments or giver of sermons. An almost overpowering motive for murder is divulged.

Though Simon Bede may not play the major role in each book, and though at times his vocation as a priest is down-played, what is constant in Byfield's books is a deep concern about evil—evil as it may masquerade as good, evil as it gets all tangled up with good, evil as people fight with temptation and sometimes succumb, sometimes not. All through her books, Byfield is interested in religious questions. How can we live a good life? What causes a good man or woman to go off the path of good and become evil? What are the unexpected consequences of seemingly inadvertent actions, good or evil? These and other religious questions are asked, implicitly and explicitly, in Byfield's books.

The Rev. C.P. "Con" Randolph

From a background of many years in the Methodist ministry and an already successful writing career, Charles Merrill Smith created the Rev. C.P. "Con" Randolph as the first Protestant minister-detective outside of the Anglican tradition.

Smith approached his task with tongue-in-cheek humor, which he had used in his best-selling *How to Become a Bishop Without Being Religious* and other witty books on aspects of Christianity. When he retired early because of ill-health, he decided to try his hand at the detective novel.

Randolph is a complex character. Young and handsome, he has been a star quarterback for the Los Angeles Rams; he's gone through the "Jocks for Jesus" syndrome and come out the other side; he was a brilliant student at seminary and went on to teach church history there. When the series begins, his friend Bishop Freddie—whose last name we never do get to know—has persuaded him to take advantage of his sabbatical year and be an interim pastor at the Church of the Good Shepherd in Chicago.

Here is another large church located in the heart of a large city. It's founders had built on valuable Loop property; people of another day, recognizing the value of their property, tore down the old structure and built an office and hotel tower, of which the first three floors became the church, topping it all off with a spire, in which the luxurious parsonage was later housed. Unlike St. Anselm's, Good Shepherd is not involved directly in ministering to the hungry and homeless; unlike St. Jude's, it has a substantial endowment and no money worries. It has become a status church for the wealthy of the Gold Coast and the suburbs to belong to if not attend, and the "in" place for tourists and conventioneers to visit on Sunday mornings. Its congregation is a floating one, its members rarely geographically close to its building. Like the other large churches it has a large staff, devoted members, and a governing board not always devoted to the minister currently in charge.

In his first year there, Randolph faces problems that are not unusual when a long-term pastor retires. One of the ministerial staff feels that he's been promised the top job and resents Randolph. The Board of Governors is unwilling to listen to the new, untried minister. There is some finagling going on with church funds, and other kinds of shenanigans going on in the choir room. The secretary who really runs the church can't transfer her loyalty from the old beloved pastor to the new one. Out of these difficult situations comes murder. And Randolph turns into an amateur detective.

In the course of the novel Randolph's circle of friends comes into being; they are the ones who will stay with him through the remainder of the series. Samantha "Sam" Stack, popular TV talk-show hostess and more than a friend to Randolph; Dan Gantry, youth minister at Good Shepherd; Lt. Michael Casey, of the Chicago police force. Others will join them as time goes on, especially Clarence Higbee, the delightful British butler/chef, who cooks up delicious meals in the parsonage kitchen and honors Bishop Freddie with the title "M'Lud."

Smith's career in the ministry and his knowledge of main-line Christianity and of Judeo-Christian history give authentic background material for the series. He worked on the theory that readers like to learn something about occupations other than their own, and so he told, in considerable detail, about the many activities of the ministry. Randolph writes columns for the church newsletter, marries people, visits hospital patients, counsels those in pain, chooses hymns, decides what to preach on and writes his sermons, says the blessing at various civic events, meets with committees and the governing board, and so on, almost ad infinitum. These are the realities of any parish clergyperson's job. Anyone considering the ministry as a career could do worse than read the Randolph books to see what it's really like—except for the murders. Somehow Randolph manages to run into a lot of them, and that's not routine in the lives of most clergy.

Though Randolph takes part in some community activities, his approach to ministry is basically personal. This involves him with a Mafia gangster in one book, with a movie starlet in another, with an apparently poverty-stricken old man living in a broken-down old house near downtown Chicago in another. He muses about sin and wonders if he's committing the sin of gluttony by eating and enjoying Clarence's marvelous meals. He delights in amorous adventures with "Sam," who becomes his wife, and lets us know that he believes that sex is a wonderful gift of God, to be enjoyed wholeheartedly. Sex in these books is happy sex, monogamous sex, somewhat ribald but always a joy for both people. There is no sadism or masochism in these tales, except where cruelty is linked with murder. Even then it is not connected to sexual behavior. Nor is violence celebrated; it is described briefly but not gloried in.

C.M. Smith died in 1985. His last book, *Rev. Randolph and the Splendid Samaritan*, was almost complete, and it was finished by Smith's son, Terrence Lore Smith, also a writer of novels. The series will continue with Terrence Smith as author, under the general title, "Charles Merrill Smith's Rev. Randolph."

IV. The Rabbis

Rabbi David Small

Rabbi Small was the first of the contemporary clerical detectives to appear on the scene, and he's had the longest run. Starting in 1964 with *Friday the Rabbi Slept Late*, author Harry Kemelman has written a book for each day of the week plus two, the most recent being *One Fine Day the Rabbi Bought a Cross.* Kemelman is not himself a rabbi, but he is a practicing religious Jew, very knowledgeable about matters of religion and tradition. His intent in these books is not only to write interesting whodunits but also to convey information about Judaism in a nondidactic manner.

At the outset readers met the young rabbi and his wife, Miriam, toward the end of their first year at a Conservative synagogue in an affluent suburban town, Barnard's Crossing. There is s prosperous Jewish community in the town, made up of people of all shades of religious practice, from nonobservant to

Orthodox. Some take Judaism very seriously; others join the synagogue mainly for contacts with other Jews. Naturally, what they want in a rabbi varies also.

Rabbi Small has been brought to the synagogue by some of the older, more traditional men. He is a scholar, a third-generation rabbi, steeped in the tradition of what rabbis were in the past, in Europe. He sees his role as that of a judge, who applies Talmudic wisdom to the tangled affairs of his congregants. Some of them would much prefer him to be like the glad-handing Protestant ministers who are highly visible in the community, but that is not his way.

He is a man of the utmost integrity; often he seems too straitlaced and traditional to his congregants, but he won't deviate an inch from what he believes to be right, even to ensure his job. He will not perform a wedding for a Jewish woman and a non-Jewish man, even though her father is president of the congregation; he will not allow a non-kosher caterer to prepare the food for the wedding reception for another couple in the synagogue; he will not bless the boats, a pleasant but meaningless tradition recently thought up by the town's selectmen. He won't even ask for a salary increase as the Smalls' two children become teenagers, nor will he curry favor with a faction in order to get someone else to get him a salary increase. Sometimes he seems to readers a very stiff-necked man, but he is always acting out of conviction. At times, though, even Miriam and the children, Jonathan and Hepzibah, get exasperated with his adamant positions!

In each book there is a crime and a painful dilemma involving someone in the Jewish community. In each book Rabbi Small is able, usually by careful reasoning, to clear the Jewish suspect and find the actual perpetrator. In the very first book the body of a young au pair girl is found on the temple grounds; she was pregnant. Suspicion centers on a Jewish man who had picked her up on the previous night; when he is cleared by the rabbi's efforts, the rabbi himself becomes the chief suspect. In the course of this investigation the rabbi meets and becomes friends with Chief of Police Hugh Lanigan, a Roman Catholic. The two men like and respect each other; their conversations give the rabbi many opportunities to expound on Judaism.

Rabbi Small works on an annual-contract basis; each year his tenure must be voted on by the governing board. In each book some group makes an effort to get the rabbi out; this sets the stage for a conflict which ends temporarily when the rabbi solves yet another mysterious crime. Usually someone in the dissident group, or connected with it, is accused and must be cleared, as in the first book. Since the rabbi has been instrumental in clearing the wrongfully accused person, he winds up with the respect of the dissidents. And so his job is safe for another year, until another book.

Barnard's Crossing is the scene of most of the books; however, the Smalls do make two trips to Israel and find that serious crime occurs there, too. In one book the rabbi teaches a course in Jewish Philosophy at a small college in Boston; he has a similar experience there. In the latter case, *Tuesday the Rabbi Saw Red*, he saves a Jewish professor from trial for murder and along the way makes friends of his rebellious students. At the same time he imparts both to students and to readers a great deal of information about Jewish history and thought.

Someday the Rabbi Will Leave is typical of the Rabbi Small books, as in this one he has to oppose the millionaire president of the synagogue. As this man has just gotten David a large and greatly needed salary increase, the rabbi's integrity is tested. As always, it comes out whole.

In the most recent book, *One Find Day the Rabbi Bought a Cross*, the Smalls make their second trip to Israel, to stay with Miriam's Aunt Gittel in her large apartment. Again the rabbi is innocently drawn into a murder investigation. The book's cast of characters includes persons representing several of the warring factions in the Middle East today. Its setting in Jerusalem allows the author to give readers some insight into the complex religio-political situation there. The rabbi, how-ever, is concerned with human beings, not with politics. As usual, he manages to offend some of his congregants while trying to help others.

Kemelman has also written a non-mystery featuring Rabbi Small, *Conversations with Rabbi Small*. It is a handbook of questions and answers about Judaism in fictional form. The very thin story line concerns a young person who wishes to convert to Judaism in order to marry a Jew.

There now should be no lack of other kinds of "days" about which Kemelman can write Rabbi Small stories. Jonathan and Hepzibah can grow up, perhaps marry, and get into dilem-mas of their own. Barnard's Crossing will continue to be a hotbed of intrigues regarding the rabbi. And, between them, Hugh Lanigan and David Small will nip any incipient crime wave in the bud.

Rabbi Daniel Winter

Daniel Winter is rabbi of a Conservative synagogue in Los Angeles. The newest entry in the growing number of clerical detectives, he was created by Joseph Telushkin, who intends that *The Unorthodox Murder of Rabbi Wahl* will be the first of a series. Winter is, on the surface at least, the kind of rabbi the Jews of Barnard's Crossing would love to have. Young, personable, author of a popular book, *The Religious Manifesto* (notable for not being entitled *The Jewish Manifesto*), he is also moderator of a radio program called "Religion and You." The program features guests who speak on contemporary issues, and a call-in time. The rabbi is plain Mr. Winter on the radio.

Still, he is definitely a rabbi, and a Conservative, even an Orthodox one at times. He keeps a kosher home; he is firm about the required language of the marriage ceremony; he walks to and from the synagogue on the Sabbath. In other ways, however, he has moved with the times. He no longer says the blessing thanking God that he's not a woman; one of the topics of his radio program is feminism and religion; and he is willing to find words for the bride to say which keep the marriage service from sounding sexist.

In this first book, widower Winter meets divorcee Brenda Goldstein, police psychologist, mother of a lively young daughter, and a nominal member of the synagogue. Ms. Goldstein is introduced as an indignant mother, for someone has stolen a valuable watch from her daughter during a religious school class. Like Rabbi Small, Rabbi Winter is skilled at handling such crises, and he wins Brenda's respect and liking. Soon Brenda and Daniel are a team, both romantically and professionally.

Myra Wahl, the rabbi of the book's title, is a young assistant at the Reform temple who has made herself decidedly unpopular by her radical ideas and aggressive feminism. So unpopular that she is about to be fired. Her personal life, too, is in sad shape. She has left a lover behind in New York in order to take this position, and she is haunted by the knowledge that she cannot live a lesbian life-style and still be a rabbi. As a guest on Daniel's radio program, along with a nun and a woman Protestant minister, she is embittered, hurt, and angry. In a vehement difference of opinion with Winter, she calls him something any Jew would find hard to forgive. So, when she is found the next morning, murdered, he is one of the suspects.

Lt. Cerezzi, Brenda's boss, collects evidence from several sources and comes up with a man who must have been the killer. A prominent member of the Jewish community, president of the Reform temple, he is nonetheless vulnerable to special knowledge that Myra Wahl gained about him while counseling his daughter. Brenda and Daniel don't agree with Cerezzi, and their view is vindicated by the evidence they come up with and by another murder.

The everyday routine of a rabbi's life plays little part in this book, nor does Rabbi Winter's congregation enter into the plot. The cast comes from a wider population, the Jewish ones mostly from the Reform temple. However, the satisfactions of the work of the rabbinate are displayed as Daniel has to decide whether or not to accept the offer of the radio station to be a full-time talk-show host.

The murders are solved, not by any special knowledge of Judaism, as would probably be the case if Rabbi Small were involved, but by Daniel's careful attention to the details of what he has seen and heard. This is what makes for successful detection; this ability should serve Rabbi Winter well as he goes on to other cases. No doubt Brenda and her daughter Jessica will also appear in future cases. The combination of a rabbi and a police psychologist has to be a winner!

V. Conclusion

Since the basic theme of the mystery novel is the battle of good against evil, it seems quite natural that clergy should sometimes take the starring role of detective. It is, after all, their job to strengthen the side of the good so that evil may be vanquished. That is exactly what these clerical detectives try to do, with considerable success. They are not stereotypes; they do not make a special virtue out of church or synagogue-going; they do not urge readers to "be good for goodness sake"; they are not engaged in saving readers' souls. They offer compassion, mercy, sometimes forgiveness, often understanding, to those who have fallen off the narrow way. But they can be stern; to those who have chosen evil as their good, they bring justice.

Some of the authors make a point of providing readers with information about their religious institutions. Those who read Kemelman's books will learn a great deal about Judaism, its tradition and its current practice. Telushkin seems to be following that model. The books of McInerny and Kienzle give two quite different views of the Roman Catholic Church, each valid, each interesting for those who would know more about the ways of that church in America today. Holland's books show clearly the challenges of the very large city for a large Protestant church, though those challenges are by no means limited to the Episcopalians. Smith's books tell us how one large city church operates today, but he especially shows the daily life of a minister, which, in its essentials, is similar in both city and rural circumstances.

However interesting all that an author has to say about church, synagogue, and culture may be, in the final analysis these books must be judged on their success as mysteries. Each book contains at least one murder. Each member of the clergy works at being an amateur detective. There are no divine revelations, not even any inspired guesses. There may be a little intuition now and then, but that happens to lay detectives, too. Although the quality of the books varies, and readers will find their personal favorites and, probably, some they can't stand, the clergy operate in the best amateur-detective tradition. Generally they work in cooperation with the police. They use close observation, skillful questioning, and solid reasoning in coming to their conclusions. At times they have special knowledge because of their work and their religious backgrounds; other than that, they have no particular advantages.

Taken overall, these books make an important point. Clergy these days are deeply involved in what is going on in the world; they are not segregated from it. They, too, know its fascinations and its temptations. They wear no haloes; they understand people because they, too, are human. They apply religious precepts without being judgmental. We may like them or not, accept their religious points of view or not. As mystery readers, all we're asked to do is read and enjoy.

The Honorable Charlie Mortdecai: An Oxymoron

William F. Deeck

The Hon. Charlie Mortdecai appears in three picaresque novels by Kyril Bonfiglioli. In chronological order, but not in order of publication, they are *Mortdecai's Endgame*[1] (winner of the 1974 John Creasey Memorial Award under the title *Don't Point That Thing at Me*), *After You with the Pistol*,[2] and *Something Nasty in the Woodshed*.[3]

Bonfiglioli also wrote *All the Tea in China*,[4] which Doubleday on the jacket of *After You with the Pistol* claims to be a novel featuring Mortdecai. Well, we all know and forgive publishers their little inaccuracies; they are far too busy publishing novels to take time to read them. *All the Tea in China* is indeed a picaresque novel, but it takes place in the 1840s, and Mortdecai, who is touchy about his age, would be in a real snit if anyone thought he was of such advanced years. The book relates the adventures of an ancestor of Mortdecai's, Carolus Mortdecai Van Cleef, who also is no better than he should be. Nonetheless, it is well worth reading.

On the publication of Bonfiglioli's first novel, his U.S. publisher described him as about the same age, height, and weight as Mortdecai, also an art dealer, and possessing similar tastes and talents. Up to that time, however, he, Bonfiglioli, had not killed anyone, or so we are assured.

The novels are comparable to what one would imagine that, if one is capable of imagining such a thing, P.G. Wodehouse would have produced, assuming he had been given to depravity and unwholesomeness. Bonfiglioli does not hide the Wodehouse connection. Each of the novels has a significant number of references to the works of the Master. At one point, Mortdecai mentions that he, like the Woosters, has a code. Unfortunately,

---

[1]Weidenfled, 1972, as *Don't Point That Thing at Me*; Simon and Schuster, 1973.

[2]Secker, 1979; Doubleday, 1980.

[3]Macmillan (London), 1976.

[4]Pantheon, 1978; Secker, 1978.

he doesn't clarify that code.

Bonfiglioli's works are rich in incident, plot, and verbal felicities, and the following descriptions are at best a broad overview, and at worst don't come close to doing the novels justice. The temptation to quote from almost every page of the three novels has been sternly resisted, else the article would be significantly longer than it is.

The Hon. Charlie Mortdecai, or so says *Mortdecai's Endgame*, is the second son of Bernard, First Baron Mortdecai of Silverdale in the County Palatine of Lancaster. Mortdecai's father had gotten his barony, it was thought, by donating a lot of art to the nation, but it appeared to be bestowed for forgetting something embarrassing about a high personage. Baron Mortdecai begat Charlie on a Christmas night of a year that Charlie does not reveal; he apologized to Charlie by explaining that he was drunk at the time.

Although Mortdecai seems to have no interest in the peerage, and quite detests his brother, Robin, Second Baron Mortdecai, he is quite happy with his last name since it provides "a touch of ancientry, a hint of Jewry, a whiff of corruption—no collector can resist crossing swords with a dealer called Mortdecai, for God's sake."

For Mortdecai is a dealer in art—some genuine, some faked, some stolen. He doesn't work too hard at any aspect of it, unless his undergoing torture can be called work. Also, among other things, Mortdecai is in his mid to late forties, slightly overweight, a gastronome, a boozer, a lecher at least in word, a self-admitted snivelling coward, a traducer of women, and a fop. "Idle, intelligent, devious; a survivor," reads Mortdecai's last school report—perhaps from the "goodish second-rate Public School" he attended, the one that was "long on sodomy and things but a bit short on the straight bat, honor and other expensive extras." Years later he claims: "I have not changed; I am no butterfly."

Mortdecai's sexual life is somewhat uncertain in the first of his chronicled adventures, with sly remarks about homosexuality predominating. As his life grows more hectic, however, he seems to be thoroughly heterosexual, though frequently reluctant or pretending to reluctance to engage in sex. Apparently he talks about deviance because he wishes to shock, or at least annoy.

Chez Mortdecai consists only of his thug Jock, the type every art dealer needs, says Mortdecai, whose last name Mortdecai can't remember but suspects it's Jock's mother's. Jock is a "sort of anti-Jeeves: silent, resourceful, respectful even, when the mood takes him, but sort of drunk all the time, really, and fond of smashing people's faces in." Besides the nasty work, Jock is also chief cook, at which he is excellent, and bottle washer, level of skills unknown, for the Mortdecai household.

There is also a Mrs. Spon, somewhere in her sixties, who comes in to do the redecorating when Mortdecai requires it, and likes to play rummy and "gotcha" with Mortdecai in bed.

Presumably Mrs. Spon is responsible for decorating his bedroom, "a pretty faithful reconstruction of the business premises of an expensive whore of the Directoire period." There is also a concierge, but she plays a minimal role and is rather unpleasant, so she shall be passed by.

Mortdecai has a painting by Goya, stolen by someone or other from Spain, which he needs to get to a rich collector in the U.S. so that he may be paid fifty thousand pounds. To make the smuggling a success, he becomes involved in a blackmail scheme with the rich collector and a chap named Hockbottle Gloag, who has been up to some naughty things with somebody of importance and of the same sex and has the pictures to prove it. Hockbottle isn't around long because of an untimely demise, but Mortdecai soldiers on.

Things go wrong, as they tend to do when Mortdecai is involved, although it's not always his fault, and he finds the SPG--a secret branch of the police with very special powers, including torture and killing, the outfit that disposed of good old Hockbottle--after him in the form of an old schoolmate, Martland. Something involving a car battery and testicles--the former, Martland's, the latter, Mortdecai's--takes place, but being the recipient of the unpleasantness in pursuit of fifty thousand pounds is something Mortdecai accepts as part of an art dealer's life.

Also, by agreeing to kill his rich client once the picture is delivered, thus obviating the blackmail of the unnamed personage, Mortdecai is left to do his thing--well, temporarily, about which he has no doubts. In return for Mortdecai's promise to commit murder, Martland arranges things so that he will be able to transport under diplomatic seal a restored Rolls Royce Silver Ghost that the millionaire has purchased. The Rolls will, of course, contain the painting.

In the U.S., Mortdecai drives the Silver Ghost from Washington, D.C., to the estate of his client in New Mexico with various diverting adventures and droll comments about the country taking place along the way.

Mortdecai arrives in New Mexico to find that his client is dead, maybe murdered. Also, his client's widow, an oversexed baggage, falls in love with him. There are other problems looming, and it's time to call in Jock, Mortdecai figures, because things are beginning to look even sticklier than they had been.

The plot, as Mortdecai probably would not put it, thickens apace. The Rolls is wrecked, various unkindly people don't care whether Mortdecai lives or dies, and Mortdecai and Jock have to scurry back to England and go into hiding. Even there, or especially there, they have to go on the run again, and Jock is sucked into a bog with no hope of rescue. He asks Mortdecai to kill him quickly, and Mortdecai puts the boot in and pushes Jock under.

All that is left for Mortdecai is the painting for which he never got his fifty thousand pounds, and awaiting his end. Martland, and apparently others, are out to get him. He is certain he can kill Martland, but then someone will undoubtedly kill him. The novel ends with Mortdecai thinking: "I shall fall

like a bright exhalation in the evening down to hell where there
is no art and no alcohol, for this is, after all, quite a moral
tale. You see that, don't you?"

Those readers who keenly noted that there were three
books in the series and that the one dealt with above was the
first chronologically no doubt are suffering no undue anxiety
about Mortdecai's continued survival, and rightly so.

Colonel Blucher, who played an obscure bit role in the
first book, appears at the last minute to save Mortdecai's life in
After You with the Pistol, though not Martland's, whom
Mortdecai empties a pistol into. It seems that Blucher wants
Mortdecai alive so that he can marry the relict—the oversexed
baggage mentioned above—of his late rich client, and the relict
wants to marry Mortdecai, who wants no part of it. Upon being
told it's his life or wedded bliss, however, he bites the bullet.
Mortdecai is, as has been pointed out, a survivor.

The only good thing that happens to Mortdecai at this
point is that his thug Jock shows up, hale and hearty but minus
one eyeball where Mortdecai had kicked him in the head. Jock,
of course, takes this in his stride as all part of the game.

The bride of Mortdecai asks him a favor—after all, what
are husbands for—the day after the wedding: To kindly assas-
sinate Queen Elizabeth II. Mortdecai tries to talk Jock into
doing it, but Jock is a patriot and will have no part of it.
Mortdecai undertakes to do it himself and plots well, but when
he has the lady in his sights, he discovers that someone has at
the last moment hocused his cartridges. A good thing, too, for
Mortdecai, as we discover later, else the adventures of Mortdecai would have ended there.

His wife is just a bit perturbed at this and other evidences
of Mortdecai's feebleness, who was in one of those "joke and
dagger" outfits in World War II but is obviously out of practice.
She sends him to Dingley Dell, a school primarily for young
ladies to learn how to "Kill/Maim/Cheat/Lie/Deceive/Sub-
vert/Communicate/Bewilder/Terrorize/Persuade/Forge/Imperson-
ate/Evade/Explode/Compromise and do all sorts of other horrid
things to other people." Mortdecai's mood at the time, however,
is such that the pamphlet on "Mastering Five Simple Ways of
Suicide (three of them almost painless)" is what appeals.

Strange things happen at the school and away from it that
don't have a great deal to do with anything, and then Mortdecai
is sent, disguised as a Jesuit priest, to China—well, Macao,
actually—where he is to get something from a dentist, the inscrutable Lo Fang Hi, who really is inscrutable after some tor-
turers have their way with him.

Mortdecai does manage to collect the something from the
dentist—drugs, of course—and then it's off to Chicago, where
Mortdecai has to escape the clutches of a mysterious Chinaman
and discovers that his wife has had implanted in him a tiny
explosive capsule when all the time he thought he was having a
vasectomy ("'Good God,' I cried, appalled. 'I might have had a
baby!'"). In Washington, D.C., Mortdecai has to evade the
clutches of a mysterious American and a bunch of schoolgirls.

Finally it's back to England, where Mortdecai is caught

smuggling a piece of stolen art he didn't know he had. After his arrest, he tries to remain in jail so that all, and that's a great number and, who knows, may even include the schoolgirls, who wish to kill him may not do so. Thrown out of jail, Mortdecai romps through an abattoir pursued by those who desire that he become one with the slaughtered pigs. Jock, fortunately, arrives in time.

If you think all this is a bit much, imagine how Mortdecai felt. Fortunately, in the next episode, *Something Nasty in the Woodshed*, Mortdecai does little traveling. He and his oversexed wife and his thug Jock are living on the Isle of Jersey until Mortdecai's numerous enemies have a chance to calm down after his previous misadventures.

Unpleasantness seems to follow Mortdecai wherever he goes, however, no matter how hard he tries to avoid it. A series of rather more than nasty rapes occurs in the parish in which Mortdecai lives, several of which happen to the wives of acquaintances of his. From the descriptions of the rapist and some investigations Mortdecai makes, it appears that Satanism has reared its ugly head.

Mortdecai's friends want to guard the homes of possible rape victims so that they may catch the rapist in the act, maybe even before, and Mortdecai, grousing as usual, falls in with this. But he also, as is his wont, has to make something more of the circumstances. He toddles off to consult experts on Satanism, figuring that he might as well fight evil with evil, no particular surprise when Mortdecai is involved.

Mortdecai gets hold of an unfrocked priest so that a Black Mass can be held threatening the Satanistic rapist with his own master. It is a very amusing and also tragic performance and leads to Mortdecai and friends being incarcerated, albeit temporarily.

The rapes, though horrible, are treated by Mortdecai in his usual droll fashion, something which will drive feminists, as if Mortdecai cares, right round the bend. They will be somewhat mollified to discover that the rapist, catching Mortdecai off guard while he is on guard as it were, nails the poor chap's ear, with the poor chap still attached to it, to a tree.

All does not come out well in the end, and Mortdecai demonstrates that even he has feelings. But whether he is shedding tears for his friends or for his deceased canary we apparently shall never know. For thus it seems endeth the chronicles of one of the lesser but most amusing anti-heroes.

The Cream of Queen

Frank Floyd

MAY-JUNE

William Bankier, "Oil and Water" (June)

"Career Move" by D.R. Benson is a nice light burglar tale, colloquial in style. While the plot of Thomas Adcock's "Cracker Jack" has been used before and the development is melodramatic, the ending won't leave your emotions untouched. "The Teddy Bear" and "The Stamp," both authored by Isaac Asimov, are for those of us who like a mental challenge. Dr. Asimov writes by the KISS method, and his stories give an easy and pleasant satisfaction. "The Teddy Bear" and "Stamp" also provoke ideas on odd human behavior and on the blind spot in the thinking process which causes people to cling unwisely to a false line of reasoning.

Stories by William Bankier have appeared regularly in EQMM in recent years. On the whole they are above average. But "Oil and Water" is where he really puts it all together. Here he has written a story which fills the numerous stringent demands made of the modern mystery short story—originality, character, unobtrusive plot, relevance, consistency, and universality of appeal.

Stacey Berenson, the producer of a weekly situation comedy, is bored by doing over and over something which no longer is interesting to him. Then he meets Curtiss K. Norman, a street-corner violinist, and Curtiss's sister Freda, a couple of free-living unpredictables. They are immediate tonic for Berenson. However, about sunup the next day they wind up in a house on the ocean-front, along with the body of Freda's much older husband, a wealthy financier and lover of young women, who has been living in the house with Bethany Lieberman—young, female, reasonable price tag—and Freda has been brooding about it.

This is a short story for people who don't like short stories. Most readers of "mystery novels only" will appreciate it. Dislikers are far too often the sad outcome of the difficulty writers have in generating universality of appeal while fulfilling at the same time the other demands of the form. "Oil and Water" does, which is an achievement to be underlined.

JULY-AUGUST

John Mortimer, "Rumpole and the Younger Generation" (August)

Mystery Fanciers, astute as they are about their favorite kind of reading, may wonder whether I am less fault-finding when dealing with the stories that I review than I ought to be. Some explaining would seem in order.

First, the story featured is selected from twenty or more by some of the best writers in the United States, Great Britain, Japan, and other countries and is apt to be very good. And, second, the short story's position in the marketplace is precarious, and I do not care to fall in with its defamers by drawing undue attention to poorer stories, even if only to point out their shortcomings. What I do is to take these things into consideration when I make my selection. The purpose of this column is the bringing of a story you might think good to your attention, rather than the listing of the transgressions of a writer sinning against sense in form or logic.

This time I came down to a choice between "Jojo and the Tethered Goat" by Jeffry Scott and "Rumpole and the Younger Generation" by John Mortimer. I decided the praise for Rumpole has been well meted out.

"Rumpole and the Younger Generation" is the first Rumpole that Mortimer wrote. The crotchety old barrister defends a young teen-aged boy whose family's family tradition is crime. Meanwhile, Rumpole realizes some things about himself and about his own son. And we, the readers, learn that She Who Must Be Obeyed is a name that fits. Rumpole tries to justify his decision to remain an Old Bailey barrister for the rest of his years in Chambers, a decision unpopular with She, misunderstood in Chambers, and materially unrewarding.

Guaranteed! If you would like a few chuckles and have not got around to George Baxt's "Adamant Eve," a spoof--the characters are not quite like those in *Gone with the Wind*--you should get around to it.

It's About Crime

Marvin Lachman

For over five hundred years, the history of Richard III has fascinated historians as well as lay people. Proof of this is publication of the third book on the subject printed within the last two years. (The previous books, one fictional: Guy Townsend's *To Prove a Villain*, and one factual: Audrey Williamson's *The Mystery of the Princes*,[1] were previously reviewed in this column.) Mysterious Press has reprinted another novel based on the case, Elizabeth Peter's *The Murders of Richard III* (1974) in paperback for $3.50. This book, which is about what Peters calls "the most fascinating, frustrating unsolved murder in history," features one of here series characters, librarian Jacqueline Kirby, whose acerbic qualities would have made the young Katherine Hepburn ideal to play her on the screen. Kirby and a friend, an American professor named Thomas Carter, are in London and are invited to a weekend house party given by a group of adherents of Richard III in Yorkshire. It's a cross between a Bouchercon (call it a Richardcon) and a science fiction convention, with panel discussions and people dressing up in costume, albeit of the fifteenth century.

The book has been well researched, though it is loaded in favor of the Richardist viewpoint, probably reflecting the author's sympathies, certainly those of her characters. Refreshing is some speculation on Richard's mistress and his own bastards. The plot has some surprises, and the clues are presented fairly so that the reader can guess, even if Kirby claims that here solution "wasn't deduction; it was a crazy hunch." Despite that, Peters lets Kirby's explanation go on far too long; it consumes ten percent of the books 230 pages. Still, the action moves crisply and Kirby and Carter make an interesting team, with him playing Watson to her somewhat abusive Holmes.

I can't prove there are more *characters* living in small British villages than elsewhere in the world, but reading mystery

---

[1]*Editor's note: I must take exception to Marv's characterization of these two books, since there is more fact in my "fictional" work than there is in Williamson's allegedly "factual" work.*

fiction makes me suspect so.   Certainly Robert Barnard's *A Little Local Murder* (1976), reprinted by Dell at $3.50, adds weight to that belief.   Barnard gives us a village called "Twytching" and a devastatingly funny picture of its local residents.   A British radio station has come to Twytching to do a documentary broadcast, and they let some skeletons out of the closet, bringing out the worst in people—and causing murder. Showing another side to his writing, Barnard makes us care quite a bit about the murder victim.   This is close to Barnard at his best, and that is very good indeed.

Bargains are few nowadays, but Signet has provided one with a reprint of all twenty-two Sherlock Holmes stories which have appeared on PBS's *Mystery!* in the last few years.   Their edition, complete with a cover evocative of Holmes's time, has 533 pages and sells for $3.50, the exact price asked by another publisher which recently reprinted only the seven stories in the latest TV series.   There's also Frederick Busch's excellent introduction to recommend Signet's edition, but the main attraction as always is the atmosphere and Holmes-Watson interplay created by Doyle.   If it is true (as I believe) that Holmes is the most recognized character in the history of fiction, it is with justification.

Punny titles are among the earmarks of writers who got their start at the pulps, as did William P. McGivern, and his *Very Cold for May* (1950) is an example once we learn that the name of the corpse is May Laval.   The setting is McGivern's home town, Chicago.   (He would later in his career write primarily of Philadelphia, New York, and California.)   May had been planning to publish a "tell-all" diary, and public relations expert Jake Harrison is hired to protect his friend Dan Riordan. When May's lips and pen are permanently sealed, he turns detective to protect himself as well as his friend.   If this book isn't McGivern at his peak (as he is in *Odds Against Tomorrow* and *The Big Heat*), it is nonetheless a lively, tightly plotted book, and Penguin deserves thanks for reprinting it (price: $5.95) in their new Classic Crime series.

Dick Lochte's *Sleeping Dog* (1985) has been reprinted by Warner for $3.50, and it features Serendipity Dahlquist and Leo G. Bloodworth, "a spunky little miss and case-hardened private shamus."   Serendipity is only fourteen, a 1980's version of Holden Caulfield.   When she and Leo find a corpse, she is blase, not queasy, saying, " I've seen dead people before, tons of 'em. On TV."   This unlikely team works together in a wild, fast-moving mystery about such unlikely subjects as dog-fighting and television.   The Southern California scene, used so often in the past, has seldom been better portrayed, with an especially devastating picture of the ocean town, Playa del Rey.   Equally good is Lochte's picture of Bloodworth's car: "It had dark tinted windows, the better to hide behind.   Its back seat was covered with jackets, sweaters, strange hats, brown paper bags, squashed into balls, Big Mac wrappers, greasy fried chicken boxes, and empty beer cans.   It was the car of a dedicated, working gumshoe."

The Bride Wore Black (1940; reprinted by Ballantine, $2.25) is Cornell Woolrich's first novel and has been reprinted by about half a dozen different paperback houses. If you've never read Woolrich, it is a splendid introduction, and the Ballantine edition may still be available, although it first appeared in 1984. While it is not Woolrich at his very best (for that, you'd have to read pulp novelets like "Goodbye, New York" or later books like *Rendezvous in Black*, also reprinted by Ballantine), it is very good indeed. Woolrich is best known for his heart-stopping suspense, emotional prose, and use of outrageous coincidences. In *The Bride Wore Black*, we have his usual narrative drive, but the language is a bit more objective than it sometimes is, and the result is a bit less reader involvement than is needed. The coincidences are there, in spades, and that makes suspending disbelief a bit tougher than usual. Still, only someone who's read the *best* Woolrich would dare to cavil at this book, so don't miss it if you've never read it.

John Dickson Carr was living in South Carolina when he died, so it is somewhat fitting that the last Gideon Fell mystery, *Dark of the Moon* (1967; reprinted by Carroll & Graf, $3.50), should be set in that state. A deviously plotted mystery, with its roots going back to the Civil War and even two centuries before, is only part of the attraction here. This is a book of many contrasts: ghosts are prominent, yet there is the fair play detection we expect from Carr. There is the spooky atmosphere of an old Southern mansion, and yet there is a hilarious baseball game, reminiscent of the time Carr/Dickson gave us Sir Henry Merrivale at bat in *A Graveyard to Let*. Finally, there is Fell, English to the core, having to function in hot weather in the U.S., after arriving in the South in his typical "shovel hat and a black cloak as big as a tent."

Also from Carroll & Graf, a publisher which is doing some of the most interesting reprints lately, is Nicholas Blake's *Murder with Malice*, $3.95. This is yet another title for the book which began life in 1940 as *Malice in Wonderland* (easily its best title) and was reprinted in the United States the same year as *The Summer Camp Mystery*. In 1964 Pyramid reprinted it as *Malice with Murder*. Oh well, as Gary Hart probably once said, "What's in a name?" Under any title, this is one of the best examples of the late Golden Age of classic puzzles that you'll find in paperback. Nigel Strangeways is called to investigate strange doings at a holiday camp named Wonderland, where a series of practical jokes—e.g., tennis balls dipped in treacle—by someone who calls himself "The Mad Hatter" have culminated in murder. The humor is sophisticated and the puzzle very difficult to solve. The setting is believable but far enough removed from our usual lives to make perfect escape reading.

Some books date very quickly; an example is Sarah Shankman's 1985 *Impersonal Attractions*, reprinted by Paperjacks, $3.50. Annie Tannenbaum, free-lance writer in San Francisco, is researching a book about single people who advertise to meet each other through ads in the "personals" columns of the newspapers. She is not averse to meeting "Mr. Right" herself. When she places her own ad she has both purposes in mind. Unfortunately, a Jack-the-Ripper sex killer is currently preying on women in the city. (The hardcover publisher tastelessly advertised: " ... there are straight men in San Francisco; One of them is a mass murderer!") What Annie did when this book was written was foolhardy enough, but now, only a couple of years later, it would be sheer lunacy because of the AIDS crisis. We have Annie and the killer "Meeting Cute" (to use the title of her proposed book), and there is a great deal of excitement in a fast-paced book which, nonetheless, is shallow and predictable.

There is much in Shankman's book that is not for the squeamish, and the same can be said regarding John Collee's *Kingsley's Touch* (1985; reprinted by Penguin, $3.95) about an Edinburgh surgeon who seems to have developed the ability to cure cancer with a single touch. This is partly a medical novel, with realistic descriptions, and partly a violent thriller. It has too many elements of the fantastic to appeal to this reviewer or, I suspect, to the editor of the magazine you are now reading.

Several columns ago I review Sue Grafton's third Kinsey Millhone mystery, *"C" Is for Corpse* (1986) when it was in hardcover; Bantam has now reprinted it at $3.50. This is a book in the best traditions of the Southern California private eye mystery, but it is as up to date (and timeless) as all good examples of the sub-genre. However, some reviewers have so praised Grafton that the incautious reader may expect that she has broken new ground in the field. Not so, but she's a solid storyteller who has created an interesting detective in the Lew Archer tradition.

THE BEST MYSTERY SHORT STORIES OF 1986

There are many mystery fans, including readers of *The Mystery Fancier*, who don't read *any* short stories. While I like novels just as much, I read about four hundred short stories what were published in 1986. This consisted of every issue of *EQMM*, *AHMM*, *Espionage*, *New Black Mask*, and *Hardboiled*. I also read two original anthologies, *Ellery Queen's Prime Crimes #4*, edited by Eleanor Sullivan, which consisted of twenty-five short stories never previously published in the U.S., and *Mean Streets*, the second PWA anthology, edited by Robert J. Randisi and published by Mysterious Press in hardcover. I also read a handful of other stories in publications like *Mystery Scene*, *Redbook*, et al. While I am sure I missed some, I'd say I read enough to make the following annotated list, which shows the stories in the order of my preference.

1. Isak Romnu, "Love Is Here to Stay" (*Espionage*, October 1986). For those who like spy stories (and even for those who don't), the "mole" story to end all "mole" stories. The single most enjoyable story of the year.

2. Clark Howard, "Scalplock" (EQMM, July 1986). Another example of his powerful writing as he integrates the subject of AIDS into the mystery format. Howard was the only writer to

appear with two stories on my list.

3. James Powell, "The Origami Moose" (EQMM, June 1986). Bumbling Sgt. Bullock returns to prove mystery and mirth can mix very nicely.

4. Linda Haldeman, "Shabby Little Shocker" (AHMM, July 1986). The most sophisticated story of the year, about the world of opera, with a beautifully ironic ending.

5. John H. Dircks, "Algorithm 512" (AHMM, December 1986). A science-fiction sounding title, but really a medical detective story, featuring the latest in modern technology.

6. Clark Howard, "The Wide Loop" (EQMM, October 1986). Modern-day cattle rustling in Montana, coupled with Howard's special insight into the world of the underdog.

7. Charles Naccarato, "Who Dares Tell the President?" (*Espionage*, December 1986). A scary story about international politics with a plausibility that won't help you to sleep more easily at night.

8. Doug Allyn, "Homecoming" (AHMM, mid-December 1986). A moving story which captures Northern Michigan, its people and its climate.

9. Fred Hamlin, "The Clam Soup Collection" (AHMM, August 1986). A public defender and his 19-year-old defendant who is accused of a hitchhiking murder. Two believable protagonists in a compassionate story.

10. Edward Wellen, "Backup" (*Espionage*, June 1986). Industrial espionage in a clever science-fiction mystery that will appeal to all punsters.

11. Celia Fremlin, "The Sensory Deprivation Tank" (EQMM, March 1986). Medicine again (psychiatry) and some of the most suspenseful moments of the year.

12. Ron Goulart, "Monster of the Maze" (*Espionage*, February 1986). A wild and wacky Harry Challenger story set in 1896.

13. Stephen Wasylyk, "The Stainless Steel Cart" (AHMM, January 1986). A likable hero and the most unusual weapon of the year.

14. Adam Hall, "Last Rites" (*Espionage*, April 1986). The perfect length for Quiller; suspense and terrorism at sea.

15. Bill Crenshaw, "Tide in the Affairs" (AHMM, June 1986). Adam Clay, reluctantly on vacation at the beach (" ... sandwiches with real sand"), finds an obnoxious brother-in-law and crime awaiting him.

16. William Bankier, "Information Leading to" (EQMM, March 1986). The Canadian-British author goes just a bit out of control on this one, but the puns and action make it thoroughly worthwhile.

DEATH OF A MYSTERY WRITER

No, this is not a review of the Robert Barnard mystery of the same title, but rather a resumption of the periodic lists I used to include in this column, before its sabbatical, of losses we have suffered in the field.

PEGGY BACON, on 4 January 1987 in Kennebunk, Maine, at age ninety-one. Though best known as an artist and illustrator of more than sixty books, Bacon also published a mystery, *The Inward Eye* (1952), reprinted by Mercury as *Lady Marked for Murder*.

FRANKLIN BANDY, on 11 April 1987 in White Planes, New York, at age seventy-two. A former director and executive vice-president of the MWA, Bandy won that organization's Edgar as best paperback original novelist in 1976 for *Deceit and Deadly Lies*.

FRED DICKENSON, on 6 May 1986 in Sarasota, Florida, at age seventy-seven. As a young newspaper reporter, Dickenson had reported on the Chicago gangland slayings known as the St. Valentine's Day Massacre. For over thirty years, beginning in 1952, he wrote the story for the "Rip Kirby" detective comic strip. He had published one mystery, *Kill 'em with Kindness* (1950).

BERNHARDT HURWOOD, on 23 January 1987 in New York City at age sixty. He wrote on a variety of subjects, with titles such as *Writing Becomes Electronic: Successful Authors Tell How They Write in the Age of the Computer* and *The Whole Sex Catalogue*. He also wrote *My Savage Muse*, an imaginary autobiography of Edgar Allan Poe. Hurwood wrote two mysteries, *Rip-off!* (1952), a Gold Medal paperback original, and *Born Innocent* (1975), the novelization of the movie. He once served on the board of directors of MWA.

RICHARD LEVINSON, on 12 March 1987 in Los Angeles at age fifty-two. With William Link he had created the phenomenally successful television series *Columbo* and *Murder, She Wrote*. They had also written the *Mannix* and 1976 *Ellery Queen* TV series. For their work, they won a record total of four MWA Edgars. Link and Levinson first began collaborating when they were in junior high school. In 1954, when Levinson was only twenty, they won a prize in *Ellery Queen's Mystery Magazine* for one of the best first stories of the year with "Whistle While You Work." They also appeared frequently in *Alfred Hitchcock's Mystery Magazine*.

ALISTAIR MACLEAN, on 22 February 1987 in Munich, West Germany, at age sixty-four. Beginning with *H.M.S. Ulysses* in 1956, he wrote many exciting novels. His first book was based on his own experience sailing in the Arctic convoys of World War II. Two of his most successful books, *The Guns of Navarrone* and *Ice Station Zebra*, were successfully filmed. His most recent book, *Santorini*, was published posthumously.

JOHN D. MACDONALD, on 28 December 1986 in Milwaukee, Wisconsin, at age seventy. There are probably few readers of TMF unaware of the passing of one of the greats in the field, the creator of Travis McGee and author of hundreds of pulp stories and dozens of paperback original mysteries. The McGee books became so successful that what had originally started out as a paperback series became a series of hardcovers which regularly made the best-seller list.

DWIGHT TAYLOR, on 31 December 1986 in Woodland Hills, California, at age eighty-four. As a screenwriter he wrote many mystery films, including *I Wake up Screaming, Nightmare*, and *Conflict.* He wrote television scripts for *Climax, 77 Sunset Strip*, and *Batman* among other shows.

LEE WRIGHT on 7 December 1986 in New York City at age eighty-two. One of the most famous mystery editors of all time, Wright originated the Inner Sanctum Mystery line for Simon and Schuster in the early 1940s. In 1956 she joined Random House, from which she retired in 1977, though she continued there as an independent editor. Donald Westlake, Stanley Ellin, and Ira Levin were among the authors who were first published under her editorship. She edited several excellent anthologies of mystery short stories for Pocket Books in the 1940s and 1950s.

MYSTERY MOSTS: PLAYS

Beginning in 1863 with Tom Taylor's mellerdrammer, *The Ticket of Leave Man*, which when novelized seventy years later by Cecil Henry Bullivant gave us the hero's name (Hawkshaw) as one of the synonyms for "detective," mystery on stage has been important. Conan Doyle's plays included the first serious one about Sherlock, Gillette wrote the definitive one there and other significant ones including *Secret Service*, Mr. and Mrs. North had their stage appearance, and Dame Agatha's record shattering *The Mousetrap* is so much common knowledge as to preclude one of these little essays dealing with the longest-running mystery play. However, the question remains--who did the most mystery plays?

Wall Spence published nine mystery plays in the 1930s, most of them "full-length" three act ones, but nothing else. Wouldn't it be nice if someone who also wrote books outdid that score?

Well, Ira Levin has done more mystery plays than mystery books (including some very fine ones in each field). He may eventually write more plays than Spence. Agatha Christie, along with her staggering total of books (and their even more staggering popularity) turned out a full dozen mystery plays. Edgar Wallace, whose prolificity in books needs no mention, did twenty-six plays in all; at least fifteen of them were mysteries, and the total may be as high as twenty.

But the real champion is surely James Reach, author of four mystery books and thirty-six mystery plays under his own name, and producing more in each category under his three pennames. Like Dame Agatha, he occasionally adapts his prose work for the stage, and his best play may have been the one of the same name based on his very good novel, *The Innocent One* (Coward, 1953). I have neither read nor seen any of his plays, and I further admit that this essay has been based solely on such reference books as Hubin's *Bibliography*, Reilly's *Twentieth Century Crime and Mystery Writers*, and the Steinbrunner and Penzler *Encyclopedia.* Corrections and addenda from the readers would be appreciated. (Jeff Banks)

Reel Murders

Walter Albert

Cinevent '87

Although the complexion of the dealers' room is beginning to change as the video vendors turn out in greater numbers, the programing continues to reflect the sensible mix of silent and sound films (coming no closer to the present than the mid-forties) that has characterized this convention since I first began attending it in the late nineteen-seventies.

"The Penguin Pool Murder" (1932; directed by George Archainbaud) is based on the popular Stuart Palmer Hildegarde Withers series and was the first of three films to star the redoubtable Edna Mae Oliver as the spinster amateur detective. I thought it a very appealing film indeed, but when I mentioned my enjoyment of the film to a friend he observed that he had erased it from a tape, expunging this "poorly paced" Withers/ Piper collaboration, but preserving for posterity (and me, perhaps, at a later date) a "superior" later entry in the series. I liked the film for the fizzy chemistry between Edna Mae Oliver and Inspector Pepper, played with his usual engaging asperity by James Gleason, and what seemed to my bemused eyes to be a nicely paced comedy-mystery with some Oscar-worthy histrionics by a talented penguin. But I must confess that when it comes to Edna Mae Oliver I am a patsy in the throes of an unrequited passion. (My favorite Oliver performance is in John Ford's "Drums Along the Mohawk," where she plays a feisty widow putting Indians to rout with a broom and a stentorian voice until an arrow terminates her terroristic cavorting. The only contemporary actress I can compare her to in the effect she has on me is pint-sized Linda Hunt, who conveys more intelligence and sympathy with a look than most actresses do with a pageful of dialogue. I enjoyed her un-anchored--by the script--performance in "Silverado," where amid the clutter of this entertaining shot-'em-up [and down], she displays a purity of character and demeanor that raises most of her scenes to a level to which little else in the film aspires.) However, I will delay my definitive judgment on PPM until I have seen the other Oliver/Gleason collaborations in the series.

Performance generally was superior to direction and script

in most of the films I saw that weekend. Film historian William Everson was, for the second year, very much in evidence at the convention and his interest in the British mellers was respons- ible for two films, an unscheduled postwar noir, "Wanted for Murder" (1945), an earnest film which included a fine perform- ance by Stanley Holloway, and "They Drive by Night" (1938, directed by Ernest Woods), of which only the title made its way across the Atlantic for the American remake. In the first half of the film, Emlyn Williams is a recently released convict trying to evade the police, who believe he has murdered his former girl friend. Much of this is shot at night, in the rain, and is a taut chase in the Fritz Lang vein. In the second half of the film, Williams and a new girl friend set a trap for the real "mad sex killer" (in Everson's pithy description) who is played by Ernest Thesiger, the unforgettable Dr. Pretorious of James Whale's "Bride of Frankenstein." The style clashes irreconcilably in the two sections of the film, but the casting and a nicely designed and staged scene in a period dance hall give the film some interest.

There was also an entertaining early James Cagney film, "Lady Killer" (1934; directed by Roy Del Ruth). Cagney plays a movie usher who, after a brief fling at an initially successful life of crime, goes to L.A. where he breaks into the movies and becomes a major star. His old crime buddies show up and his career seems headed for the rocks until a last-minute chase traps the bad guys and vindicates Cagney. A year earlier, Barbara Stanwyck stared in "Baby Face" (directed by Alfred E. Green), the sordid tale of a girl from the wrong side of the tracks who rises to kept affluence in a series of bedroom maneuvers that redefine the term "permissible risque." There's a redemptive finale (which Stanwyck plays with a notable lack of conviction), but her hard-boiled, terse acting in this seventy- minute film are riveting. There is a bit by John Wayne as one of the "Johns" she loves and dumps, while the other men in her life include Douglish Dumbrille, Donald Cook, and George Brent. Puzzle of the week: who plays the man she finally really falls for and for whom she turns "good"? (This is like figuring out the murderer on the Angela Landsbury "Murder, She Wrote" series. Out of all the has-beens and never-weres drafted for roles, who is the most unlikely and therefore most likely suspect?) The role is tightly circumscribed, but within the assigned limits Stanwyck is superb. The more I see of her early work (and the American Movie Classics cable channel has shown several of her lesser thirties films), the more I am impressed by her. And then there is her unforgettable acting in "Double Indemnity" (finally released on video) to crown a career that in recent years has shown all of the professionalism of this fine actress but with little of the distinctive beauty and intelligence of her early work.

There was, perhaps, one film at the convention in which acting, script, and direction combined in an often unforgettable combination: Todd Browning's "The Unholy Three," starring Lon

Chaney, Victor MacLaglen, and, memorably, the fine midget
actor, Harry Earles. This is the 1925 silent version. Chaney
plays a side-show ventriloquist (Professor Echo) who engineers a
scam in which he, strongman Hercules (McLaglen), and Tweedle-
dee (Earles) gain entry to homes of the rich who are clients of
a pet store where the trio's foil, Mae Busch, works. Chaney,
disguised as Busch's grandmother, and Earles as a year-old baby,
make service calls to treat "ailing" parrots who, once they have
left the store, cannot talk. Earles is a malevolent presence who
fully justifies W.C. Fields' wariness toward children, and
McLaglen, at moments, in makeup and hulking movements bears
a striking resemblance to Karloff's Frankenstein monster.
Eventually, a sentimental ending weakens the somber power of
the best scenes, but this is still a striking film, with a vein of
nastiness that gives it an acerbic edge sixty years after its
production.

MYSTERY MOSTS: PROLIFICITY

A given that everyone knows is that John Creasey was the
most prolific mystery novelist ever. But what writer produced
the most books about a single character? Creasey had about a
dozen series, but the longest of them stopped around twenty
books.
Erle Stanley Gardner's name will occur to most. He did a
very respectable eighty-two Perry Masons, but that is far from
a record. Several more than one hundred Doc Savage novels by
"Keneth Robeson" have appeared in book form, most of them
written by Lester Dent. Walter B. Gibsonm usually writing
under the house name Maswell Grant, did over two hundred
novel length adventures of the Shadow, but only about forty
(including reprints and new adventures) of the Shadow books are
by him. Both Doc Savage and the Shadow were Street and
Smith plup heroes.
That was the same fiction factory company that produced
the champion of them all. Frederick Van Renssalaer Dey
published over four hundred Nick Carter stories (mostly in S&S
dime novels); his 203 dime novels include 187 about Carter. No
one else comes close to that mark, and only Gibson would seem
to have the potential to ever do so. (Jeff Banks)

Verdicts

(Book Reviews)

John Rhode. *Poison for One.* Dodd, Mead, 1934.

There are times when only a classic puzzler from the Golden Age can hit the spot for the mystery lover. It has to have names like Gerald, Muriel, Percy, and Rupert, a country house with a few guests, a strange murder, a baffled Scotland Yard man, and a non-professional detective who solves the case while rarely moving from his armchair. Add that the Yard man be Superintendent Hanslet and the benign intelligence to whom he defers be Dr. Priestly, and you have *Poison for One*, guaranteed to fill that spot with warm satisfaction.

When Sir Gerald Uppingham is found dead in his locked study, a bottle of cough medicine laced with prussic acid nearby, Superintendent Hanslet of Scotland Yard is called in. Uppingham was a wealthy financier; among his guests were Lord and Lady Cossington and two directors of an Uppingham-led firm, British Albanium. Coincidentally, the firm produces cyanide as a by-product of its manufacturing. The method of murder seems obvious and motives abound. Sir Gerald has made a number of people angry by his persistent pursuit of women. His fiancee, Muriel Featherleigh, daughter of the impoverished Cossingtons, is reluctant to marry him. His sister, Elvira, will be put out of her home and forced to live on a small income upon his marriage. One of the directors frequently goes to the works and could have possessed himself of the wherewithal to poison Sir Gerald; furthermore, he seems to have something to hide, as does his wife.

Mysterious circumstances abound. A stranger has phoned Sir Gerald from the inn on the night of the death, and then has disappeared and cannot be traced. Another phone call may or may not have taken place. The cork from an inferior bottle of wine is found on the study floor. The doctor is very attentive to the bereaved fiancee, and the secretary to the bereaved sister.

As is his custom, Hanslet tells Dr. Priestley about the case. Priestley, his secretary, Harold Merefield, and their friend Dr. Oldham are fixtures in Rhodes's books. Priestly is a retired scientist and a fount of knowledge about many subjects. With kind condescension he suggests avenues of investigation that

Hanslet has not considered, blinded as he is by his conviction that one man is the murderer. When all his assumptions are overthrown, Hanslet has to turn his ideas upside-down and meekly follow Dr. Priestley as, by evidence and intuition, he arrives at the right conclusion.

The British class system, upheld by the invisible bounds of different kinds of education, is encapsulated by Oldham's smile when Hanslet does not understand his reference to "Timeo Danae ...". Hanslet has not had a classical education. (Maryell Cleary)

Alison Smith. *Someone Else's Grave.* St. Martin's, 1984, 192 pp.

What do you get when you combine *Our Town* with a murder mystery? *Someone Else's Grave*, of course.

Alison Smith has written a folksy murder mystery set in a small New England town where all the victims, suspects, and investigators live together in happy oblivion.

Her plot structure is superior in its use of multiple suspects, but in the end you will know whodunit before the name is revealed to Judd Springfield, chief of police in Coolidge Corners.

I liked the texture of this book more than the plot. It feels good. There are no surprises, really, but the layering of characterization and small-town color make this a satisfying experience for the reader.

All in all, it's quick reading of a comfortable, passable nature. (Alan S. Mosier)

Simon Brett. *Not Dead, Only Resting.* Scribner's, 1984.

This is the tenth in Simon Brett's Charles Paris series, and as usual it is full of black humor and unfavorable reviews.

Charles Paris is an actor, you see, who is perpetually down on his luck. He is again in this book. He's out of work, what the British acting profession refers to as "resting," hence the title.

Paris solves the murder mystery about two lovers that own a restaurant in his usual stumbling fashion. If only he were as lucky in his acting as he seems to be in his sleuthing!

Simon Brett is a witty author who writes on the cutting edge of sarcasm. His parodies of the stage are first rate, and his pacing is, for the most part, fluid. He does sometimes play unfairly with the dispersal of evidence to the reader, making it difficult to reach the solution before Charles Paris, but, this aside, *Not Dead* lives up to its nine precursors. (Alan S. Mosier)

Allen J. Hubin. *Crime Fiction, 1749–1980: A Comprehensive Bibliography.* Garland, 1984, 712 pp.

Detective fiction, the step-child of literature, has emerged as a bona fide genre, with growing recognition and respect.

No longer do teenagers hide in the closet with a cops-and-robbers paperback. Major universities are beginning to offer courses in the history, trends, and aesthetics of suspense fiction. And distinguished publications are dedicated to the appreciation of works in the field.

Until recently, the cornerstone books of critical essays about the mystery-crime-detective story were Howard Haycraft's *Murder for Pleasure* (1941) and *The Art of the Mystery Story* (1946), Herbert Brean's *Mystery Writer's Handbook* (1956), and Francis M. Nevins' *Mystery Writer's Art* (1971).

Among the pioneering bibliographies in the genre were *The Detective Short Story* (1942) and *Queen's Quorum* (1951), both by Ellery Queen; *XIX Century Fiction* (1951), by Michael Sadleir; and *Victorian Detective Fiction* (1966), by Dorothy Glover and Graham Greene.

During the last decade the floodgates have opened and many new publications came out to shed light on the Classical Puzzle, the Hardboiled School, the Police Procedural, International Intrigue, and other subgenres in the arena of literary crimes.

Crime Fiction, 1749-1980, a bibliography by Allen J. Hubin, was issued recently by Garland Publishing and overnight became the most important reference work in the field. It is the end result of a monumental effort to catalogue, in one massive volume, more than a century of adult fiction in which, according to the compiler, "crime or the threat of crime is a major plot element."

Within 712 pages, three columns per page, Allen J. Hubin has accumulated English language mystery, detective, suspense, thriller, gothic, police, and spy fiction, published in book form--both soft and hard covers--since the middle of the eighteenth century.

From Voltaire's *Zadig* (1749) to *The Prose Romances of Edgar A. Poe* (1843), through the Sherlock Holmes tales by Arthur Conan Doyle at the turn of the twentieth century into the Golden Age of Agatha Christie, S.S. VanDine, and Ellery Queen during the twenties and thirties, and the hardboiled revolution of Dashiell Hammett and Raymond Chandler, culminating in the modern era of Bill Pronzini, Edward D. Hoch, and Robert Ludlum--they are all included here.

The main body of the bibliography consists of the Author Index, to which all other sections refer. Here all the authors identified with crime fiction published through the end of 1980 are arranged in alphabetical order (from Patrick Aalber and Edward Aarons to Edgar Zukas and Eva Zumwalt). Books are listed alphabetically under the byline. Cross-referencing is provided to the author's real name, where different from the byline, and to any other pseudonyms used.

The headlines to bylines entries provide author birth and death dates. They also identify series characters ("protagonists recurring in two or more books").

The books listed under each byline are normally rendered with their first American publisher and date of first U.S.

publication and/or their first British publisher and date of first British publication, "depending on whether the books were published in both countries."

The nature of the book content is also defined. Collections of short stories, collections of novelets, plays (with number of acts), criminous book-length poetry, translations, and novelizations of stage, radio, TV, or motion pictures (with the original source given) are identified.

The Author Index is followed by a Title Index which lists, alphabetically, all titles and relates them to the byline under which they first appeared (from *ABC Affair* by P. Winston to *Zylgrahoff* by J.C. Shannon).

As if that was not enough, *Crime Fiction, 1749-1980* also contains a Settings Index which lists geographical locales (from Abyssinia to Zurich, Switzerland) and specialized settings like Academia (examples: I. Asimov's *Death Dealers* and G.D.H. Cole's *Scandal at School*), Aircraft (C.D. King's *Obelists Fly High* and W. LeQueux's *Terror in the Air*), Church (G.A. Birmingham's *Hymn Tune Mystery*), Hospital (C. Brand's *Green for Danger*), Trains (A. Christie's *Murder on the Orient Express*), Ships (N. Carter's *Sea Trap*), and Theatre (H. Traubel's *Metropolitan Opera Murders*).

The industrious editor then adds a Series Index in which all series characters are listed alphabetically, and a Series Character Chronology where they are categorized according to one of the following types:

* Adventurer ("a character who acts out of love for intrigue or danger or revenge, rather than primarily for a fee; a knight-errant")--The Four Just Men, created by Edgar Wallace; Charteris's Simon Templar, "The Saint."

* Amateur ("a character whose activity--detection, primarily--arises out of abundant 'accidental' encounters with crime and corpses, and who takes no fee")--among others, Father Brown by G.K. Chesterton and Jane Marple by A. Christie.

* Criminal--Arsene Lupin by M. Leblanc and Dr. Fu Manchu by S. Rohmer.

* Police ("a member of a local, state, or national law enforcement agency")--Charlie Chan by E.D. Biggers and Lt. Valcour by R. King.

* Private ("an investigator who seeks clients and takes a fee; a private eye or lawyer")--Sherlock Holmes by A.C. Doyle, Nero Wolfe by R. Stout.

* Spy--Mr. Moto by J.P. Marquand, James Bond by I. Fleming.

Utilizing his own library of some 25,000 blood-and-thunder volumes, consulting milestone reference works like *A Catalogue of Crime* and *The Encyclopedia of Mystery and Detection*, and incorporating information supplied by knowledgeable readers and authors in the field, Allen J. Hubin has accomplished the Herculean task of collating 60,000 titles into a comprehensive bibliography of crime fiction. It is an admirable, landmark achievement. (Amnon Kabatchnik)

E.C.R. Lorac. *I Could Murder Her.* Doubleday, 1951; Collins, 1951, as *Murder of a Martinet*; Popular Library, no date, 191 pages.

Muriel Farrington is a domineering woman who, unfortunately for them, has her entire family living with her in her stately home. She tries, often successfully, to run the lives of her children, her stepchildren, her in-laws, and her husband, and she seems to be despised by all except her husband and one son.

When she is found dead one morning in her bed, the family doctor, who is old, ill, and hasn't be very able for years, is unable to attend and bestow a certificate, which he would have done without investigation or thought. A younger, more able and perceptive doctor has to be called in, to the shock of whoever the murderer was, and he does not find the death natural. A hypodermic puncture in her arm leads him to believe, correctly as it turns out, that someone has injected insulin into the woman. Since she was not suffering from diabetes, death was the inevitable result.

The characterizations of those in the household are well done, particularly the one of Mrs. Pinks, the charwoman. The motives of each of the family members who may have killed Muriel Farrington are set forth clearly.

The investigator, Chief Inspector Macdonald of the C.I.D., a continuing character in many of Lorac's novels, is not very distinct, however. He is quiet, kind, considerate, and an excellent investigator in his own way, but that's all that is learned about him. Perhaps Lorac had delineated Macdonald in his earlier cases. Nonetheless, she could have taken a little more effort here to acquaint new readers with him.

A fairish-play novel. The murderer was evident to me, and I don't spot too many. The clues are psychological rather than physical. (William F. Deeck)

The Documents in the Case

(Letters)

From Otto Penzler, The Mysterious Empire, 129 West 56th
Street, New York, NY 10019:

This time, you've gone too far. I can handle it if you
knock my taste in literature. It's no problem if you attack my
political stance. I find it bearable if you condemn me for
arrogance or for a dull personality. I have no trouble sleeping
if you don't like the way I dress. I've never complained when
you bad-mouthed the city I live in and love. But to snidely
remark on my height (or lack thereof) is more than a man can
stand (and I am standing, damn it). If I am cut, do I not
bleed? Oh, dark day, when you have to stoop so low as to
refer to my height. This I can never forgive.
Apart from that, all best wishes.
[*Gee, Otto, I don't recall ever saying you had a dull
personality.*]

From Maryell Cleary, Box 155, Lyons, OH 43533:

I enjoyed the last TMF. Particularly Bill Deeck's "Further
Gems"; lots of chuckles there. Lots of good stuff in Marv
Lachman's "It's About Crime," too. With all the multitudes of
mysteries about nurses, doctors, and hospitals, you'd think
there'd be more set in psychiatric hospitals, wouldn't you? Yet
I can't think of any. Helen McCloy did have a psychiatrist
detective, Basil Willing, but so far as I recall he operated
outside of a hospital. As for Richard III, long may the con-
troversy wave. It gives us good mysteries and a good puzzle to
mull over.

From Marv Lachman, 34 Yorkshire Drive, Suffern, NY 10901:

Vol. 9 No. 2 has everything: poignancy in Ely Liebow's
reminiscences of John Nieminski, facts in Jeff Banks's material;
a superb article about Boucher's work by Joe Christopher; humor
in Bill Deeck's quotes. It even had praise of yours truly by
Bill, and I hope I deserve it. Finally, we saw the editor

practicing what he preaches by allowing me a forum to continue to question the guilt of Richard III.   No, Guy, I'm not a Richardist, just an agnostic on the subject.   I'm glad that you are willing to defend to the death my right to sit on the fence. If *To Prove a Villain* did not totally convince me, it made me doubt Tey, so it must have been pretty convincing in its own way.   More important, it provided me with a really good mystery.   As Ira Gershwin said: "Who could ask for anything more."

Back to Deeck and his letter, interesting as always.   I understand that Richard Stevenson, in a recent mystery, has his protagonist worrying about AIDS.   Like Deeck, I could do with *less* about the sex lives of detectives in the books I read, and I hope that Mr. Stevenson will practice safe mystery writing in the future.

Bill also asks whether the reprinting of so many old books indicates something about the quality of today's books.   As is my wont, I'll give a straight answer and say, "Yes and No!"   I suspect that lapsing of copyrights may have something to do with reprinting of books by Freeman, Wallace, and A.E.W. Mason.   Legal beagles Nevins and Townsend can probably comment more about that.   [*Certainly Nevins is eminently qualified to comment thereon, but Townsend wouldn't dare.*]   I think there is a lot of fine stuff now being published, though if I were on that famous desert island and had to choose, I would certainly opt for the classic puzzles.   I believe that most mystery readers, like me, want variety in their favorite escape reading.   Tired of the sex and gore in even the best of the current crop, they return to an era when writers were forced to assume that readers had imaginations. Also, writers were willing to work harder at devising puzzles, and that appeals to many readers, too.   All I can say is I am very thankful the publishers Bill Deeck has mentioned (and Harper's Perennial Library, too) continue to keep the good old stuff available.

From Joe R. Christopher, 820 Charlotte, Stephenville, TX 76401:

I received TMF 9:2 a couple of days ago.   It was very good of you to run my Boucher piece all in one issue, although it filled up much space; I really expected it to be broken into two or three installments.   I noticed two misprints in it, only one of which might cause confusion.   On page 18, line 9, your eye skipped from one *for* to another; the sentence should read: "*Exeunt Murderers* picks up Boucher's introduction *for* "Mystery for Christmas" which was written *for* the M.W.A. anthology *Crime for Two* ... " (stress on the *fors* added).   (The other typo is a period for a comma--in the first sentence of the last paragraph--but that one just makes a fragment, not a confusion.)

Now then, if the editor of *Mythlore* would just publish my "Usuform Robotics: Anthony Boucher's Future History" (which he's had since '85), if *The Armchair Detective* will publish my "A Celebration of Anthony Boucher's Detectives" (which it has only had for a year), and if I'll revise and submit somewhere my "On Anthony Boucher as a Writer of Limericks" (which Phyllis White pointed out had a big flaw in its first draft), then I'll have caught up on Boucher and be ready to write some more. (Just as soon as I get two non-fiction books done ....)

From Charles Shibuk, 2084 Bronx Park East, Bronx, NY 10462:

It's late and I'm tired, so I'm not sure whether the author or the reviewer of *The Whole Spy Catalogue* is at fault, but George Smiley was certainly not introduced in *The Spy Who Came In from the Cold*. This was Smiley's third appearance.

Jeff Banks might also note Bruce Graeme's long writing career. Graeme, the father of Roderic Jeffries (a.k.a. Jeffrey Ashford and Peter Alding), had his first book, *Blackshirt*, published in 1925. *TCC&MW* I lists two novels published in 1979. I don't know if there were any subsequent works.

From Frank Floyd, Route 3, Box 535, Berryville, AR 72616:

I don't know but would think that a great number of Mystery Fanciers still read Erle Stanley Gardner's books. All of a sudden I have become curious about which of his books are considered best. I know that besides the many Perry Mason and Donald Lamb-Bertha Cool books Gardner wrote books about several other characters, the best known of which are probably the D.A. books.

It seems that to determine Gardner's best would be a real task. I really don't have the time and resources to undertake it right now, but I still have my curiosity. So I am wondering what the Mystery Fanciers think. Do some of them have an opinion? What is Erle Stanley Gardner's best—his best books? his best series?

If a Mystery Fancier did have the time, if he did have the reference resources, I think it would make a good article. I would like to read it.

On the other hand, I hate to see Mystery Fanciers feel ill will toward each other. My own idea is that, although we might not even like each other to live around, we should, or at least it might be better for us, to put aside any personal wrath, in view of the good feelings we receive from our common interests. On this basis, I consider all Mystery Fanciers to be my friends and whatever they do and say is my concern and interests me.

[*From a later letter:*]

You will no doubt notice the shaky, wavering, etc. penmanship of this note and may not recognize it as having come from my own typewriter, but it is because of the over-wrought condition of my nerves, etc. There has been a sinister, etc., occurrence at the old house in the Metalton area near the Miller-Doss-Harp ruin, a melancholy reminder of a once-thriving country store of yesterday much frequented by long-forgotten rustics. This quaint and creaking dwelling has been the

residence of my family for time out of mind--out of my mind
(my wife says it's been about two-and-a-half years).

I have secretly determined to post this letter to you
without delay, but I hesitate, for fear what I write will be
thought the ravings of a lunatic, an unsettled mind, etc., when
circumstances cause me to doubt my own senses, especially my
own sense. How many living or dead mystery fanciers, now
reading *The Mystery Fancier*, can make the amazing statement
that their lives have been saved by Sherlock Holmes?

Just now, upon pulling open my bedroom door, I discovered
on the hall floor a three-foot snake facing in my direction. I
cast my eyes around the room for a possible weapon. My eyes
at length fell on volume II of *The Complete Sherlock Holmes*.
This is 1122 pages of mayhem, detection, and retribution, cloth-
bound, Doubleday, featuring the great consulting detective.
Taking the heavy case-book in my hand and creeping within
striking distance of the snake, I raised it and flung it violently
down on the reptile's head. This baneful creature turned belly
up and lay without motion. The vastness of Sherlock Holmes'
criminal experience had been the telling factor.

I at once called to mind the remarkable events surrounding
"The Adventure of the Speckled Band," in which Holmes was
connected with the singular affair of the venomous viper of
Stoke Moran manor house. In my own case, with a great deal
of caution I was able to learn that the snake was not real. My
son had set it for me.

Still, there have been several seemingly unrelated, etc.,
events here. Two weeks ago a member of a certain religious
sect known for its door-knocking stopped by. The woman was
in her sixties and harmless to anyone in any physical way
whatever, and yet she had hardly opened her mouth to speak
when her slip fell down around her ankles without warning--to
her or me. I attempted to explain this away by telling myself
that there were logical reasons for it to have happened; that
the woman had lost twenty-five or more pounds avoirdupois in
weight since she had last worn the slip normally; that the
elastic had stretched; that the slip had come from a yard sale
or been borrowed from a hefty friend; that the woman could
have recently coughed with a tremendous force. Then, only the
day before yesterday, my father, who lives nearby and is
retired, received three free samples of Huggies in the mail. It
would seem on first glance that Huggies merely sent the samples
to the wrong person, but the question which has been haunting
my mind since this occurred is, did Huggies in some mysterious
manner find out my father has been eating a lot of fresh
cucumber lately?

The speckled band at the present time is lying submerged
between some of the dishes my wife has in the sink. You may
depend on hearing from me if there are any further disasters at
the family seat, which may get a foot in it, I dare say.

From Jeff Banks, Box 13007 SFA Sta., Nacogdoches, TX   75962:

Congratulations on what I take to be your fiftieth issue
(counting the "prospectus" issue).   Is my count accurate?   I
must do a MM on mystery fanzines one of these days, so my
question is a serious one.

If this *is* the fiftieth issue, I would have expected something more of a celebration––or don't you count the "prospectus"
(or maybe those few issues Steve produced while you were
exiled to academe) in your personal reckoning?   [*Actually, if
you count the preview issue TMF 9:2 was the fifty-first issue––
and of course I count the issues Steve edited.   But I don't get
very excited about birthdays, anniversaries, and other similar
milestones.   Just another of my countless character flaws, I
suppose.*]

Before I stray too far from the MM subject, I'll mention I
am enclosing two more of the little essays this time.   Yes, I
know I promised three or four each time a new TMF came out,
BUT:

(1) I have already sent several more than promised
before they began to appear;

(2) my typewriter problems seem to get worse rather
than better; and

(3) both these are a tiny bit longer than the top
length originally planned and promised.

If these won't do, for length or any other reason, please
let me know.   I won't offer to cut them, as both already have
been cut considerably from their first-draft size.

I am pleased with the debut of MM; was surprised at your
using most of my query letter as an intro. for the feature, *but* I
see the editorial wisdom.

I am not pleased about *two* things connected with the
feature––both my fault.   First, here I am sending *two* more
pieces, both of them longer than I promised they would be (and
I have another about the same size in my file to send later!); I
guess I will have to revise my original letter's promise and say
that I will TRY to keep them under a page, but occasionally
they will be longer.   Of course, as mentioned earlier, you won't
make me mad if you bounce them.   Second, I have a mental
block re: *The Maltese Falcon*, one of the mistakes C. Shibuk was
kind enough to correct recently.   *Wilmer* will ever be *Wilbur* to
me.   Back in Hubin days, a published letter had the ref. cut out,
and a correction came in the mail along with some comments on
a case I was making regarding some books I thought should be
included in the Hubin Bibliog.   I have caught myself making the
same mistake (repeatedly in conversation),   Now I seem to be
developing a similar problem with one of the bigger radio stars.
This was Bennett *Kilpack*, who I find I have called "Kilpatrick"
in everything I've ever written about him.   At *least* I caught it
when I saw it in your current issue, but it still got into print.
Woe! (Or should that be "Whoa!"?)

This (fiftieth) TMF was a nice one.   Nothing in it I like as
well as Bob Sampson's pulp articles or stuff by Jim Traylor on
Spillane, but nothing I skipped reading, either.   In fact, I spent

the hour and a half after this issue came reading it cover to cover. Yes, I *do* read my own stuff (how I caught my Kilpack/Kilpatrick fluff!) but I *don't* read it first. Though, another confession, I did look on the contents page first for the MMs.

On my read I liked best the Christopher and Deeck pieces. I was also surprised to see two of my reviews in the same issue. Enjoyed the whole issue. Only—who's "God"? Could that be the writer who recently published an article on the *Spenser for Hire* series in *TV Guide*?

MYSTERY MOSTS: TCOT TITLE PATTERN

"The Case of the ..." is probably the most familiar beginning for Mysteries in the English language. At least when an American reader sees it, visions of Perry Mason overwhelming D.A. Burger and the guilty party in the courtroom, of Della, Paul, and Lt. Tragg all playing their important parts, is what springs to mind. If we visualize them in the persons of actors Burr, Tallman, etc., that is subject matter for another essay.

The British reader is quite likely to visualize Mason, too, for the books enjoyed a fine sale there, but he might think first of Christopher Bush's fifty-six books whose titles began with the same pattern. Those, and five others before them, almost the writer's entire output, featured Ludovic Peters. This hero was a wealthy amateur detective, rather a British Philo Vance. At least, if Van Dine started *his* hero helping D.A. Markham a few years before Bush began backing up Scotland Yard's Superintendent Wharton, Bush was slightly ahead of Gardner with the TCOT titles.

Gardner was certainly the most prolific, using the pattern for all of his Perry Masons, which makes him the writer who most used that pattern or any other for adventures about a single mystery character (and incidentally using it also for a very few other non-Mason books). However, few American readers will be aware that another series hero had more than twice as many books with that title pattern, though the books were written by **many different writers.** In fact, it *might not* be Bush and Peters that your typical British reader would think of *first*.

That pattern is only one of several prominently used in the tremendously long and long-running series about Sexton Blake. There it first appeared, so far as a reasonably careful bibliographic search could reveal, on a Blake book by John William Bobin. That writer did many other Blake books, including nine more with the pattern that Gardner and Mason are so identified with. Other writers working in the series, seventeen of them, had turned out almost a hundred Blake books with that title pattern before the appearance of *TCOT Velvet Claws*, so for all his prolificity, Gardner did not even match the use of *his* title pattern in another series; since the start of the Mason series, another fifteen Blake writers brought the total of books in that series with TCOT titles to 190. (Jeff Banks)

BOUCHERCON XVIII

MURDER IN THE NORTH COUNTRY

Ritz Hotel
Minneapolis, Minnesota
OCTOBER 9,10,11 1987,

Matt Scudder

GUEST OF HONOR

LAWRENCE
BLOCK

Bernie Rhodenbarr

-- Toastmasters --

Max Allan Collins & M.S. Craig

OTHERS EXPECTED TO ATTEND INCLUDE: *Bill Pronzini, Marcia Muller, Sara Paretsky, Herb Resnicow, Otto Penzler, Bill Crider, Robert J. Randisi, Linda Barnes, Allen J. Hubin, Dominick Abel, Ed Gorman, Kate Green, Edward Hunsburger, Teri White, Michael Seidman, L. A. Taylor, Doug Hornig, Francis M. Nevins Jr., Guy Townsend, Joe L. Hensley, Ruth Cavin, Warren Murphy, R. D. Zimmerman, Mary Logue, Stephen Cohen, Harold Adams, Molly Cochran, Bill DeAndrea, Barbara Michaels-Elizabeth Peters, John Lutz, Loren D. Estleman, Jonathan Gash, Ian Stuart Malcolm Gray & many more*

HIGHLIGHTS: ·· a film program, a benefit auction (for the Give the Gift of Literacy Foundation), the Anthony Awards, the PWA Awards, *a full day of alternate* **Sherlockian** *programming* with John Bennett Shaw *to celebrate the* **Sherlock Holmes** centenary; a Saturday night banquet (separate registration required), a panel of spouses · to tell *their* side; scheduled autograph sessions, the Western side of Crime Fiction; the Midwest Mystery Scene, and the Canadian Crime Scene … (**plus more**...)

Registration : $25.00 until July 1st · $35.00 thereafter …Supporting membership $10.00

WRITE: BOUCHERCON XVIII, P. O. BOX 2747, LOOP STATION, MINNEAPOLIS, MINNESOTA 55402

www.ingramcontent.com/pod-product-compliance
Lightning Source LLC
Chambersburg PA
CBHW031616040426

42452CB00006B/548